Part 1

Drowning In Numbers

I'm Just Dieting

Recovery. Anorexia. I didn't think they pertained to me. I was a dieter, not an anorexic. Dieting was in my genes. My grandmother called my mother fat more times than I can recall, and that was worse than being called anything else to mom. She would fume, she would rant about grandma behind her back, and then she would diet some more, the cabbage diet, Jenny Craig, all the diets out of Marie Claire magazine. One by one she would try them, and fail. My aunts would visit and I would hear friends and family members gossip about using the only qualifier that mattered to us; who got skinny and who got fat. 'Jenn has gotten so fat, what is she eating?' 'look at that skinny slut Teri.' 'How does Raina stay so skinny, that little bitch.' Then they would all evaluate their own bodies, 'I have gotten so fat, look how much skinnier you are, what is your secret, I need to lose so much more weight.' After these visits mom would start a new weight loss plan. She would walk miles around the neighborhood, work out double with her Richard Simmons VHS, or try not to eat altogether. It never mattered what your body actually looked like, if you were a woman you needed to lose weight.

So I became a dieter. Not an anorexic. By the time I was nine I was already unacceptable. I hated my stomach, my thighs, my arms. I didn't want anyone to see my body and desperately wished I could shrink down to be a size my family could be proud of. It took me a few more years of body hate before I tried my first diet, then my second, and on and on.

My teen years were full of trying not to eat fast food, cutting sweets, and I even tried working out with Richard Simmons. My 20's were filled with avoiding breakfast, 10 day fasts, and I even took my turn with Jenny Craig. Then came my kids, and my 30's. I went fat free, I went carb free, I bought treadmills and exercise bikes. I bought a book that had the calorie content of every food and kept it in my purse and with me always. I carried my own salad dressing everywhere. I had been dieting for decades, and without even knowing it, somewhere in there, when I wasn't looking, my dieting turned into anorexia.

My kids would tell me spinach wasn't a meal. Of course it was a meal! And a healthy one at that! My husband was concerned when I went to the gym twice on Easter; but working out is good for you so it can't be a problem. I would air fry carrot strips and put them in a leaf of romaine….hot dogs I would proudly proclaim as I topped them with mustard and low calorie ketchup...then I would serve them to everyone and be so proud of my healthy meal. The more my family tried to kindly tell me I had a problem, the more I dug my heels in in the name of health. I was finally succeeding at dieting. I was finally losing the weight, it was getting easier and easier. My daughter was begging me to stop working out all the time. My husband was pleading for me to sit and eat a real meal with him instead of eating spinach while standing. I was so angry at the people I loved the most; how could they not be proud of me? How could they not see how hard I was working to be healthy and to be the skinny me I had always dreamt of? Do they not know me at all? I was becoming more withdrawn, more infuriated with every comment they made, infuriated with their selfishness and unwillingness to see that I am doing what I love, I am dieting, I am being healthy. Eventually, for the most part, they stopped commenting. They would just look at me with sadness and fear in their eyes. I was alone with my veggies just how I wanted it.

But now I was even angrier. I was mad at them for thinking I had a problem. How dare they think I am doing anything other than being healthy and fit. I decided to show them food wasn't an issue for me, it was a choice, a healthy choice. It would be no big deal. I can eat what they eat. I can stop working out for a day. I invited my daughter to eat with me and had it all planned out; I was going to eat whatever she ate. Simple. I would do this to show her I COULD eat whatever I wanted. I COULD eat all the unhealthy options if I wanted. But something unexpected happened. The moment I invited her I felt my heart race. My mind started speeding up as well, what would she choose to eat? She loves sushi. I can handle eating sushi, although I haven't had rice in years. She also loves mac and cheese. Oh no! What if it is mac and cheese. If it is mac and cheese I will just get something else. I can't get mac and cheese, it is out of the question, simply too many calories. I mean, sushi already has too many calories, but mac and cheese, no way. Why am I getting what she is getting anyway? There is no need for that. I will just get a regular meal of my own. Something I feel like eating. What do I feel like eating? I don't even feel like eating. My brain was now non stop arguing with itself.

By the time we were in the deli I was a mess. All the foods had too many calories, were too big, too fatty. Of course, my daughter had no idea what was wrong with me because she had no inkling that I had planned to eat at all,

especially something other than salad. Then I saw the soup. I can do this! Soup! Surely there is a less scary option of soup available. I walked over to the soup counter.
Cream-of-whatever-no way, keep moving, chicken chili- too dense, clam chowder-calorie bomb, minestrone…..ok….there it is….minestrone. I can handle this. It actually sounds so very good. I haven't had beans or noodles in years either! Yum, noodles, I am so excited, I get to eat noodles. I open the lid to the minestrone and dip the ladle in to give it a stir. All of the macaroni goodness at the bottom comes swirling to the top and I immediately feel sick looking at all those calories. Even the veggies are the calorie dense ones-carrots and corn and peas. I start to pull the scoop upwards and as the ladle comes to the surface I panic, it has just too many noodles, too many beans. I dip the ladle back under and try again. I scoop up and again there are just too many bits and bobs in my scoop. I need more broth and less calories. More broth. Less calories. I find myself dipping the ladle down again, but this time tipping it until I feel all the heaviness fall out. Then I lift a scoop of almost all broth with a couple of shreds of spinach stuck to the side. I pour it into my bowl and put the ladle back. I look up to see my daughter looking at me rather annoyed.

"I love soup," I try to buffer the moment, "It's minestrone, lots of noodles and beans, mmmm."

We check out and sit with our food, her with her sushi and me with my broth. I look down worried I might see too many beans or noodles have slipped into my bowl when I notice the worst possible thing that could be wrong with it; there is oil floating on the top. It is like a greasy oil slick has fallen onto the top of my soup. My stomach sinks. How am I going to eat this with oil on it? I look at my daughter grabbing a piece of sushi with her chopsticks, dunking it into soy sauce and putting the whole piece in her mouth at once. I wish I could be that free. I THOUGHT I was that free. I THOUGHT I was in control. I thought I was choosing this healthy way of eating. But if eating this way was really my choice why would I be looking at my daughters full cheeks with envy? Why am I longing to feel her freedom to eat mouthfuls of rice and rich sauces? I decided I can do this. I can eat my soup, my broth, fat and all.

I look down at my bowl. The oil is swirling into shapes like clouds in the sky, it looks like a chicken, then a rabbit. I grab my spoon and hover it right above the slick of oil that now looks like a chicken again. The oil has settled into this shape and is no longer shifting and moving about. It has a reddish hue to it and the more I look at it, the more I can't seem to dip my spoon in. If I dip my spoon in I will disturb the oil and it will mix back into the broth. I look at the oil. I look at my spoon. I look next to my bowl and see my paper napkins. I look back at the oil. The red hue of the oil reminds me of the oil on pizza. I used to eat pizza years upon years ago and whenever I did I would blot all of that greasy oil off with a napkin. I look back at the napkin on the table and then back to the perfectly still slab of oil on top of my soup broth. Forgetting where I am, forgetting who I am with, forgetting I am in charge, I pick up my napkin. I carefully fold my napkin in half so it will fit perfectly in my bowl and I ever so gently set the napkin on top of the oil…so that it just touches the top layer and then I carefully pull the napkin back off. I set the oily wet napkin on the side of my saucer and wait for my soup to still itself again. I sit staring into my broth. As it stills I see some more oil has formed on the top, not much at all, but why leave any oil at this point. The napkin worked great! I fold another napkin, this time forming it around my pointer finger, and I dab at the oil until I feel I captured it all. I put the wet napkin with the other and stare into my bowl again waiting to see the results. The broth comes to an oilless stop. SUCCESS! The oil has been lifted! The soup is safe to eat, fat free, oil slick gone. I am feeling so proud of myself. I grab my spoon and am ready to dig in.

Then I look up. I remember where I am. I remember who I am with. My daughter is staring at me with her mouth wide open. Her hand is in the air holding a piece of sushi on the end of her chopsticks, it drips with sauce. I can feel her horror. I can feel her anger and frustration. I can feel her embarrassment. But most of all, I feel her sadness. I feel the sadness she feels for me. Her eyes say everything and so she doesn't speak. I look at my broth and try to deflect with some humor but we are both too sad now to find any of this funny. I thought I was in control. I thought I was dieting. I thought I was healthy. I was so angry at my family for coming between me and my healthy lifestyle. I was going to show them this was a choice, but they were right, it isn't a choice. I am not choosing this. I want the sushi. I want the oil. I want to feel the freedom she feels when she eats without fear. But I can't seem to choose that. Instead I choose carrot hotdogs, hours in the gym, and oilless broth. They were right all along. They were right and I want out. I want the sushi. I want the oil. I want the freedom.

"Mom, do you think you have a problem with food? Mom, do you think you have anorexia?"

I do have a problem. I do need help. I am not dieting. I
am not healthy.

"Yes, yes I do. I love you. And yes. I do."

When I Was Size 12
Tales From Childhood

When I was size 12 I was a big woman, even though I was a little girl.

When I was size 12 my thighs touched and that meant I was not deserving of love from a boy. Instead, if a boy was interested in me it meant I had his pity, not his love.

When I was a size 12 I was so heavy it felt like I ran in slow motion.

When I was size 12, my older cousin was also a size 12, and her brothers always called her fat, therefore I was fat.

When I was size 12 everyone stared at me all the time wondering why I didn't lose weight...believe me...I was trying.

When I was a size 12 I had to wear the same clothes again and again, because it was all that fit, and all that looked ok.

When I was a size 12 I was lucky to have a boyfriend.

When I was a size 12 I was the larger, chunkier sister.

When I was a size 12 every single female in my family was on a diet and most of them were SMALLER than me.

When I was size 12 a guy at a party told me my arms were HUGE.

When I was a size 12 my stomach had rolls and fat that I could not control.

When I was a size 12 I was touched more by men that were molesting me than by men that loved me.

When I was a size 12 all I wanted was to be smaller; ALL I WANTED.

When I was a size 12 I knew my father would be proud of me and love me more if I were thinner.

When I was a size 12 my skinny aunt would always point out fat people and make fun of them.

When I was a size 12 that same skinny aunt would call her sister a fat pig, I was bigger than her sister, so that made me bigger than a fat pig.

When I was a size 12 skinny was the best thing you could be in my family, skinny was better than smart, skinny was better than rich, skinny was better than kind.

When I was a size 12 I prayed to God that I could catch anorexia so I could get skinny.

When I was a size 12 I got a boyfriend and let him do anything he wanted to me.

When I was a size 12 my thighs were so big I was called thunder thighs.

When I was a size 12 all of my thoughts revolved around getting skinny.

When I was a size 12 I fasted for 12 days trying to get skinny, instead I got faint, angry, and stayed the same size.

When I was a size 12 I felt like I was less than anyone else, I was not worth the same as them, they were all better than me.

When I was size 12 my mom was a size 8, yet always, ALWAYS, trying to lose weight and be smaller.

When I was a size 12 my dad was always flirting with skinny women, even though he was married to mom.

When I was size 12 my breasts were huge and they were the only good thing I had to offer a boy.

When I was a size 12 I felt like I was in someone else's body, I wanted to climb out of my skin all of the time.

When I was a size 12 my sister was extremely skinny and everyone loved it.

When I was a size 12 I was unworthy of the time or attention of others, boys or girls.

When I was a size 12 I didn't want to be alive anymore.

When I was a size 12 I felt guilty after everything I ate.

When I was a size 12 I was embarrassed to meet anyone, I knew they would only see my size and know I was worthless.

When I was a size 12 my grandma told me I was getting fat.

When I was a size 12 I felt stiff and round and solid like a man.

When I was a size 12 I would spend the entire time I was on the beach adjusting my swim suit and towel so that my stomach didn't show.

When I was a size 12 it was clear every pair of siblings had a fat one and a skinny one and in my family I was the fat one.

When I was a size 12 my boyfriend called me fat….a lot.

When I was a size 12 I would cheat on my boyfriend to feel skinny but instead I just felt more fat and useless.

When I was size 12 I was sad.

When I was size 12 I was unloved.

When I was a size 12 my family hated people who were size 12.

When I was a size 12 I hated myself.

The Fifth Secret

There were so many recipes. One cup water, 1 Tbsp cocoa, 2 packets stevia. Mix, pour into a shallow tray and freeze. Viola! Chocolate bars. Romaine leaf, thin whole carrots, sugar free Ketchup, mustard. Air fry carrots, set one on a leaf of romaine, top with condiments. Viola! Hot dogs. Then there were the staples. Cucumbers as crackers. Mustard as cheese. Lettuce as anything bread. Stevia as sugar. Mushrooms as meat. Cauliflower as rice or oatmeal. Food was never food, food was always a replacement for food, a slight of hand per se; and that was the first secret to thinness, and I loved it. I was living the dream. I was finally there.

How many thousands upon thousands of people want what I have found, the secret to thinness? How they must look at me in the street and wish to have my slender body filled with the straight lines of bones. My life is finally what I want it to be. I am finally who I want to be, it feels good, and it feels right. My days are finally mine.

I wake up in the morning and pour my black coffee feeling superior to my husband whose weak mind forces him to add cream to make it palatable. I don't need cream, I need thin. I get ready for work and as I do I hear my husband crinkling the wrapper to the graham cracker box. I can't understand why anyone would eat in the morning. It is so counter productive to having the body that you want to have; the body that everyone wants to have. I have a second cup of black coffee, a third, and then I fill my tall portable cup with the rest of the pot before heading out the door to work.

The teacher's lounge is full of snacks and I avoid it like the plague. I never eat at work. Eating during the day is a sign of weakness and I am not weak. Eating during the day seems like a foreign activity made for other people, one that I do not understand nor do I need. When I do see someone with a handful of food I get confused. Why would they eat in front of someone else? Why would they show such slovenly personal weakness? Don't get me wrong, I like these people that I work with. I just don't understand them. Watching them eat is like watching a foreign film without subtitles, I would like to be in on the storyline but it just seems too complicated. So I just sip my coffee all day and avoid, avoid, avoid. After all, I like being thin, and to be thin I can't eat during the day, and that is the second secret to thinness.

As my work day ends I start to panic a bit because I will soon have to deal with my family. My husband and two daughters fail to understand my lifestyle, they fail to understand me. So I get my story all ready, the same story I tell every day, my new truth; "I already ate, we had a big lunch brought in today to work, I am stuffed, I couldn't possibly eat anything for hours". Sometimes they argue, but mostly they have given up, and they should give up because I am right. I know my body best and now that I have found the secrets to thinness I will not turn back because It has taken my whole life to find them, and secret number three is to always lie to protect your thinness because if you tell the truth then all of the jealous people in the world will try to talk you out of your goal, your goal of being thin.

As dinner approaches I pick one of two plans. Plan A is to avoid at all costs, start cleaning furiously, go to the gym, go for a walk, pretend to be asleep, come down with a stomach ache, anything to remove myself from the meal. Plan B is to make dinner for everyone, including a huge portion of low calorie vegetables such as broccoli, zucchini, or salad with mustard for the dressing. Then I fill my plate with the vegetables, fooling everyone into thinking I am eating dinner with them. I will always go for plan A first, but if all else fails Plan B will work nicely. This makes secret number four, always have a plan, the most necessary of the secrets because without a plan you may end up eating and that would ruin all your hard work thus far of creating a life of thinness.

Before bed I reward myself for being so good during the day. I have a giant bowl of vegetables drizzled in mustard to fill my stomach. I have a bowl of sliced cucumbers dipped in sugar-free-no-calorie syrup as dessert. I have a piece of my chocolate bar I made from the freezer to quell my cravings. Then my tummy is full and cozy and I can sleep, that is, until I get up and do it all again tomorrow.

My four secrets to success. Never eat food, only replacement food. Never eat during the day. Always lie to protect your thinness. Always have a plan. These have become the rules I live my life by. These secrets have become my scripture. And If these have become my scripture then the gym has become my church. I hesitate to call the gym one of my secrets as it is not a secret to anyone. It is always full with congregants. The gym is where I go to pray to the gods of slender. It is where I go multiple times a day, on easter, on christmas, especially on my birthday. It is where I leave my offerings of sweat and pounds of fat. It has become my safe place, my second home, and no one better try to take that away from me.

These four secrets gave me everything I have spent decades of my life yearning for. They gave me superiority. They gave me power. They gave me thinness and what I thought was sheer control. What I know now and what I didn't know then is that there is and always was a fifth secret lurking just under my awareness. Hiding somewhere between my genes and my amygdala. A secret passed on to me by my ancestors, a gift so powerful that it could someday come alive and save them all when the time was right. And this fifth secret is that the first four secrets have a name, and her name is Anorexia.

Part 2
Seeing The Light

The Rope

I slip my feet out of the heated flannel and place my toes
to the cold wood as my exhausted body tries to lift itself from
the mattress. I sit in the darkness on the edge of the bed
squeezing my eyes tightly shut trying to talk myself out of
moving any further.

"You don't have to do it. You don't have to do it." I hope
that repeating this will block the thoughts of what I have to
do. I hope that repeating this will make me forget that I have
to get up, have to check, have to know. I hope that repeating
this will finally make it ring true, "you don't have to do it."

But, somewhere deep inside I know, it does not ring true,
it never rings true, and, I do have to do it. I sit a few more
moments on the side of the bed, in the darkness, berating
myself silently. I scold myself for lying awake for 15 minutes
now, 15 minutes have gone by in which I could have already
gotten up, done what I needed to do, and gone back to bed, to
warmth, to safety, to sleep. I also chastise myself for needing
to get up in the first place, for needing to know, for needing at
all. Mostly, though, I am so angry at myself, so angry at
myself for being this fat. If I wasn't this fat I wouldn't need to
know, to check, to make sure. In fact, if I wasn't this fat I
wouldn't need anything at all, because I would already have
everything.

I lift my weak body off of the bed and begin the familiar
trek to the bathroom. I slowly creep across the floor of the
bedroom to the door trying not to creak the wood surface

below. I am sure my husband heard me slip across the floor an hour ago and I am desperate not to wake him again. Sadly, my need to know and my need to check outweigh my need to not wake him, so I keep softly tiptoeing out the bedroom door. My body temperature is lowering with every step and I am shuddering with the chill in the air. I can feel my stomach muscles clench in retaliation. The house is 70 degrees but my body does not process it that way, to my body this house is frigid, and that frigidness is trying to constantly infiltrate me, so much so that I must have all my muscles tight to ward off the cold. So I keep sneaking my way down the hallway, muscles tight, until I reach the bathroom door.

The door is closed and I put my hand on the bronze knob. I pause for a moment, as I know what is to come, and it is worth the cold. I open the door to a rush of warm wind. I stand in it, I bask in it, I feel it flush my face as I enter. Once inside I quickly and methodically close the door behind me, turning the knob as it shuts to lessen some of the inevitable noise. Then I turn around to face it. To face the object that has woken me from my sleep again. The object that has total control of my life. The object that tells me how I feel, what I do, and who I am. The scale. I am the scale. The scale is me.

It sits on the floor between the toilet and the cabinet, just centered, and the bottom edge runs perfectly along the crack that lies between the large Spanish tiles. It is of course clean and spotless, as dust adds weight. I walk up so that my toes are two inches away and look down. It looks up at me with it's hardened silver face and blank gray eyes. I have to weigh less than last time. Well, let me rephrase that, I have to weigh at least the same as last time, but my goal is to weigh less than last time. I had met my goal of being medically underweight months ago, but now there is a new goal, and the new goal is to weigh less than the last goal. This way I never have to make a new goal, the new goal makes itself.

I step on, right foot and then left, trying to get a perfect centering of each foot so that none of my weight feels unevenly distributed. I stand there attempting to keep my body as light in the air as possible, using what little core strength I have to lift my body off of the scale, in an attempt to hover over it and not actually stand on it at all. I look down. It reads precisely half a pound less than an hour ago. I have no feeling yet about this information. Half a pound less. I step backwards off of the scale and bend down to grab it by its front edge. I slide it out so slowly that it makes no noise as it slips gently across the floor and I stop when it is centered perfectly within one of the large floor tiles. Again, I stand with my toes two inches away and look down, and again, it stares up at me with it's stoic face. I try to step on with the same graceful dance as last time, but this time it does not feel soft, graceful, and light when I step up so I have to step back down and try again. On the fifth try, and after feeling my body get very much weaker, it finally feels right and I get to stay on. I pause for a moment and peer down. More than a half pound less. This time the scale is .6 pounds less. Having the scale inform me twice now that I have truly lightened I am starting to relax enough to shed the numbness that had taken over my body and I begin to feel the rush that has been released upon seeing the lower number flash in the eyes of the scale. I back off and bend down to move the scale into its third and final spot. I slide it so that the crack in the tile goes perfectly straight under the center of the scale. I repeat the process of getting on, only trying twice before staying on this time. Half a pound less again.

I step off and stand silent, just me and my scale, here in the middle of the bathroom, here in the middle of the night. I take a moment to give thanks for my lighter body. Three readings in those exact spots on the tile mean that my body has purged more weight. If even one reading is high all the low readings become false and I have gained. I ponder for a moment that I do not know who to thank for this weight loss? God? The scale? My past self for following all of the rules today as told and only eating 325 calories? Before I can figure out who to give thanks to, all of the good feelings of relief and calm are replaced with the sinking dread of how far I have left to go, of how much more I have left to lose. It is as if I am drowning and seeing the number gives me one fresh breath of air to gulp down, but as soon as I gulp it I realize I am still sinking, drowning, dying. And just like if I were alone sinking in the middle of the ocean, there is no fight to be had, there is only an acceptance of my fate, a slow descent to the oceans floor. An agreement between myself and the scale that I will not fight, because while I know I am descending into death, the descent itself feels so right, so calm, it is like a slow motion underwater ballet, but I am just an audience member, watching from the dark balcony, unable to jump in and save the damsel, to save myself.

I lift the scale up off the floor and carefully return it to its original position, making sure to line the front edge perfectly again with the tile crack. I step back and position myself in front of the mirror. I look at myself, though never at my face. I start at my collar bones, I feel them with my fingertips starting by the shoulder. I use my fingertips and thumb to push against the bone itself and run my thumb and fingers slowly from one end down to the other. I press my fingers around the top of the collar bone and my thumb around the bottom to grab the bone itself. I check to see how far my fingers can make it around the bone and one day I hope that my fingertips and thumb touch around the backside of the collarbone. Then, I make sure my pinkie finger and thumb can encircle my wrists. I check one side and then the other all the while watching myself in the mirror. Next is always my pelvis. I turn my body sideways to make sure the bones protrude farther out than my stomach. I feel every inch of them, imagining what they look like, always seeing them in my mind as crisp, white, and bleached. I touch the tops of the crests and feel how far they stick out. I close my eyes and think about how good it feels when I am driving down the road in my car and I slip my right elbow into the inside curve of my pelvis. My elbow just rests there like a broken arm in a sling. They just fit, the elbow and crest, like they were meant to hold each other. Sitting with my elbow within my pelvis is as comforting to me as being swaddled, held safe, and loved. I open my eyes and see that I am still fingering my pelvic bones, pinching my way around the edges. Finally, I reach around to my tailbone. My coccyx is the newest bone that has shown itself through my skin. I start at my lower spine and follow it down until I feel it, I am always shocked by its protrusion. It is so pronounced and I can hold the entire end of it within my fingertips. I touch around all of the bony bumps and cringe at the thought of taking a bath again. Baths were a love of mine, a daily way to combat the constant cold. Since my coccyx has made its appearance I can no longer sit in a bath without intense pain from my bone and the tub's porcelain making direct contact with each other.

I step away from the mirror and turn to look at the door. Before my brain catches up with where my body is taking me I am in the kitchen. I open the refrigerator and stare inside. I feel defeat as I close it again. I do the same with each cupboard door, open it, look inside, close it again. Finally, I lean with my backside against the counter and stare at the cupboard across from me. I feel my stomach aching for food. I feel a hollowness within me that yearns to be filled, yet oddly, at the same time this hollowness also brings me such a feeling of calm. The emptiness in my body is always equally paired with an emptiness in my mind, and an emptiness in my mind means there is no stress, no worry, no panic, and all feelings are numbed such that I can simply feel just the edges of them. This is the battle in my body, one empty hole begging to be filled while another empty hole is trying desperately to not let anything in.

"One cookie, one cookie, one cookie can't hurt, you are down, you are lighter, you deserve it, you've been good, one cookie, just one, just one, just one, just one, you deserve it, right?" My stomach is aching for something to quiet the spasms, and in this moment, before my mind can block the motion of my hands, I reach out, open the cupboard across from me and grab one of my husbands cookies from the wrapper that always sits half open. It is a Nutter Butter and I look at it in my hands. Two peanut butter cookies smushed together by a sweet peanut buttery filling inside. I feel it with my fingertips, I feel the sides and how the filling doesn't come quite to the edge of the cookies, I feel the groves and bumps that the pattern forms on the top and bottom. I feel the sandy grit of the sugar as it slides off of the cookie as I rub it. I put it up to my lips and smell it with my eyes closed. I feel the sweet smell start to rouse the calculator in my brain. The calculator starts to count the calories in sugar plus flour plus peanut butter plus eggs plus butter plus hydrogenated oil because everything good has hydrogenated oil plus...

My stomach takes over and I bite half of it off. I immediately taste. I taste the food. I taste the sweetness of sugar. I taste the richness of peanut butter and thickness of the cookie as it attempts to melt into one congealed mass in my mouth. I love it, I relish it, for a moment. For a moment it is safe. For a moment I can eat. For a moment the food can sit in my mouth and tease my stomach. But it only lasts a moment as suddenly the cookie seems to dissolve into a thousand tiny maggots. The maggots are all over my mouth climbing inside my cheeks and under my tongue. It sends a revulsion right through my core and I panic to get the maggots, the food, out of my mouth. I grab a paper towel and start spitting the goo into it. I spit and spit trying not to let any saliva filled with maggots spill down my throat. I begin wiping my tongue off with a paper towel, and then run to the sink and begin flushing my mouth out with water. I rinse and gargle over and over until I feel the flush of panic start to leave my body. As the panic leaves my body so does any strength I have left and I sink to sit on the kitchen floor. I lean there and listen to my breath trying to catch itself. I listen for any sound that my husband has woken. Mostly though, I listen to my voice, my voice that is raging loud in my head, my voice that is very angry at me for daring to put something in my mouth in the first place.

"Fucking idiot, fool, I am so fat, fat, fat, fat, fat, I do not deserve food, I do not deserve to eat, I do not deserve a cookie, how dare I, how fucking dare I put that in my mouth, I am going to weigh 10 pounds more now, I am so fat, fat, fat, fat, fat, I am worthless, I can't do anything right, I fuck everything up, I am too fat to eat anything, I will not eat tomorrow to make up for it, nothing, nothing, nothing, zero, I will not eat, I do not deserve to eat, I do not deserve to live at all, I am a fat fuck."

I know I have to get up off this floor eventually, and I desperately want to run to my heated bed next to the warm body of my husband, but at the same time I know I can't do that without first returning to the bathroom. I slowly reach up and grab for the sink's edge. I pull myself up and am hit with a wave of dizziness that almost sends me back down to the floor as my vision begins to go dark. I lean over into the sink until it passes and then stand and turn for the hall. I walk back to the bathroom pausing just outside the door to listen for sounds of movement from my bedroom, instead I hear a faint snore so I slink back into the bathroom closing the door behind me. I walk over to the scale and look at it in utter defeat.

"I can't wait until you throw that thing away," I hear my therapist's voice swirling in my head.

"The scale doesn't measure health," my dietitian's voice chimes in.

My therapist returns with, "it's time, get rid of it, you are strong Melissa."

I look down at the scale, bend over, and pick it up with both hands. I stare at it's blank face and suddenly I imagine I am somewhere else. I am Kate Winslet standing against the bow of the Titanic, only instead of Leonardo Dicaprio I have my scale. I have one arm swung out to my side just like Kate but the other is gripping my scale close to my body. The wind is whipping at my face and the stark taste of salt is on my lips. Half my body can feel the freedom of the air and all I have to do to feel it completely is drop my scale. Drop it into the ocean so that both my arms can swing wide and finally be free, free to feel, free to be open, free to be loved. A huge peaceful relief comes over my body and I slowly open my arm to release the scale. I watch as it floats light as a feather down to the ocean's surface. It hits the waves without a splash and begins to sink. I can see it just under the surface of the water, but then I notice something, something is with it, something is sinking with it. I see a thick dark line hooked on the corner of the scale and I follow it to the surface of the water and that is when I notice the rope. The ship's anchor rope is tied to the scale, and my eyes follow the rope up, up, up. I follow it up to the ship itself and over the rail behind me. I turn to see a thick spiral of rope on the ship's deck behind me, getting smaller and smaller, as the scale sinks deeper and deeper. Coming out from under the spiral of rope is the other end and my eyes follow this end as it leads right to where I stand. I don't need to look down now to know it is tied around my ankle and I accept my fate as I am tethered to this scale for eternity.

Suddenly I am overboard. I am sinking by my ankle slowly and with a deep calm that I thought couldn't exist. I think about numbers, I think about calculations, I am tallying weights and measures in my head as I slowly sink down, down, down, as it gets darker, darker, and darker. This is my underwater ballet, this is my slow descent. Then I look down at the scale below through glimpses of light from the ship above, and I see the rope tethering us together. I see the rope. I see the rope. Something sparks. Something moves. Something changes. I see the rope tethering us together. I am not the scale. The scale is not me. I am not an audience member in this deadly underwater ballet. For the first time I see the rope, I see Anorexia, I see her floating there in the ocean between the scale and I. She was always there, always twisted around my leg so gracefully, so stealthily, that I couldn't even see her, couldn't even feel her, I thought she was me. I am not the scale. I am not anorexia. I look down at my ankle and realize I can untie the rope. I can let Anorexia sink with the scale. Seeing the rope on my ankle and knowing it is not me but Anorexia I frantically dive downward and begin reaching and pulling at it. I am pulling and scratching but it is not budging. I keep sinking deeper and darker. Finally, snap, I feel one hair of the thick rope break, one little scratchy hair.

I am back in my bathroom, back with my scale, it is still in my hands, still looking up at me with it's blank eyes.

"Anorexia is not me. I am not Anorexia." I hear it in my head, but then She speaks louder, telling me to get on the scale, to stop wasting time.

"You need to check, you need to know, get on the scale, you have gained from the cookie, I am sure of it, you are too fat, you need to check, get on, get on, get on."

I set the scale on the floor. I am not Anorexia. She is not me. I turn to walk away from the scale, from the rope, from Anorexia. As I walk toward the bathroom door I feel a rush of hot emotion that is so intolerable I slow myself. Walking away from Anorexia is like turning on a waterfall of pain. With every step I take toward the door I feel the crushing feeling of being wrong, of choosing wrong, and on top of all of the wrong, is an outpouring of emotional pain so crippling I cannot walk any further toward the door. I stand frozen, but then the pain becomes unbearable and I retreat back to the scale. I step on. I do my dance. I step off. I step on again. I do my dance again. I step off again. Then I turn toward the door, "just go, just go, just go, just go."

"Twice is enough. Twice is enough. Twice is enough. Twice is enough." I am whispering aloud as I make my way out the door and to my bed. I repeat this chant as I climb in and pull up the steaming covers. Anorexia starts screaming at me that I did it wrong, that I must weigh three times, that now it doesn't count. I lie in bed for hours, afraid to move, afraid if I move I will give in, until finally sleep overtakes me.

The next morning comes and I wake up. I painfully and with great effort rise to sit on the edge of the bed. I slowly make my way to the bathroom and weigh myself three times. Even though I weigh myself three times this morning, something in my brain is different. Anorexia does not refer to me as "I" anymore, she calls me "you", and I much prefer that. I have scratched off the first fiber of the noose that is Anorexia. I see her not just underwater as I sink to my death, I see her now in the light of day. I recognize her everywhere, and I am not Anorexia, and Anorexia is not me.

When I Was Size 5

When I was size 5 no one EVER called me fat.

When I was size 5 I could wear short sleeves.

When I was size 5 my dad was proud of me.

When I was size 5 I loved my flat stomach and would rub my hands across it all of the time.

When I was a size 5 there was a gap in my thighs and seeing it in my shadow gave me comfort.

When I was a size 5 I wore a bikini on the beach and wanted everyone to see.

When I was a size 5 I was finally the skinny girl I always dreamed of being.

When I was size 5 my body fit into small spaces and it felt good to disappear.

When I was a size 5 I finally felt like I was acceptable to my family.

When I was a size 5 I could try on clothing without fear of them being too small...and the feeling I got if they were too big was wonderful.

When I was size 5 I was the smallest person in my family and I loved that.

When I was a size 5 I was finally the skinny sister. When I was size 5 I could eat food in public without shame, but I was still filled with guilt after every bite.

When I was size 5 I felt accomplished and powerful yet also ashamed and unworthy.

When I was a size 5 people would ask me if I was sick, I would say no, I was lying.

When I was a size 5 everyone stared at me wondering why I didn't gain weight, and yes, I was trying, but also, I wasn't.

When I was a size 5 I would rest my elbow inside my pelvic bone and it made me feel like I had won.

When I was a size 5 I was too small to wear my children's clothing, I was ashamed of this, but at the same time I loved it.

When I was a size 5 I was cold all of the time, not just regular cold, but the type of cold that has you clenching your muscles all day and night trying to fend off the frigid.

When I was a size 5 I noticed all skinny people and needed to be the skinniest.

When I was a size 5 I could no longer sit in a bathtub as it was too painful.

When I was a size 5 I felt like I was better than everyone, but also that I was worth nothing.

When I was size 5 my hair fell out so much my daughter asked me if I had cancer.

When I was a size 5 I was proud of my skinny body, and embarrassed by my skinny body.

When I was a size 5 I was the size I always dreamed of being but I still yearned to lose more weight.

When I was a size 5 my breasts hung off my chest like long sunken ferrets.

When I was size 5 I learned the family I grew up in is not the same as the family I have now.

When I was size 5 my own little family that I created and brought into this world could only look at me with sadness and fear.

When I was a size 5 acquaintances and friends called me skinny, but my own little family called me too skinny.

When I was a size 5 I was too tired to be a wife to my husband.

When I was a size 5 my husband prayed to God every day that I would gain weight.

When I was a size 5 my daughter put her arms around me and said, 'mom, there is nothing left of you.'

When I was a size 5 all I thought about was food, not of my family or myself, just food.

When I was size 5 I was afraid of food, ALL food, therefore all my thoughts were of fear.

When I was a size 5 I had anorexia.

When I was a size 5 I also had my own little family and they were so scared for me, they thought I was dying, I was.

When I was a size 5 I decided to fight for my family.

When I was a size 5 I decided to fight for myself.

When I was a size 5 I decided to fight for my self.

Fork In The Road

There are always two roads. The right one and the wrong one. Good and evil. The proverbial fork. It is sometimes easy to see the right way, but other times, the right way becomes so foggy and overgrown and murky that the wrong way looks like the only way left to go. So I travel down the wrong road, thinking it the only road, and that is how anorexia creeps right back in.

Every thought that I hear comes with a fork in the road. Every. Thought. All. Day. Every. Day. Let's just take the first thought I have when I wake in the morning. The moment I wake up I am met with, "coffee, I need coffee. Strong, hot, black coffee. What am I going to eat today? I think I need to eat my first meal earlier, I have been eating so late in the day lately and it feels like I shouldn't be waiting so long to eat, but I am not even hungry?" Insert fork in the road. I could commit to eating earlier in the morning but that path is overrun with thoughts of, "I am not hungry early, I have no appetite, I just want to enjoy my coffee in peace, my stomach feels full, why eat when I'm not hungry, I eat enough later in the evening anyway." All these murky thoughts keep pouring in until it feels as though the only choice is the choice to not eat earlier.

There are 1440 minutes in a day. Let's take a look at just two of them when I wake:

"Should I eat yet? What time is it even? Whew, it's early, I don't have to worry about it for hours. I mean, why eat if I'm not even hungry, or starving for that matter. What time should I eat today? Yesterday I didn't eat until 2. I should wait until 2. I wasn't even hungry then. Maybe I should be eating when I'm not hungry? That makes no sense. I eat enough every day. Do I eat enough every day? I think so. I mean, if I didn't I would lose more weight, right? So I must be eating plenty. Damn, that means if I ate earlier as well I would even gain more. That would be horrible. Of course it may be ok, I need it to be ok, I can be ok, but still I should not eat if I am not hungry and I am definitely not not not hungry. My stomach feels nothing, If I were hungry I would know it. I do feel hungry sometimes in the afternoon, that one day I was so hungry, remember? I even said out loud how hungry I was, I did feel hungry that day. Well, I do not feel that way now, I feel nothing. I will eat later, when I feel hungry. It feels good to eat when I am hungry, oooh like when I ate that bagel and cream cheese with avocado and I was so hungry that it tasted so good. Food doesn't even sound good now. I couldn't possibly take a bite of anything. I hope I am not being disordered by not eating…It is ok if I am not hungry, I mean, I will eat plenty later. Maybe I should commit to eating by noon. No, that makes no sense at all. If I am not hungry I shouldn't eat, why force food on myself when I am a perfectly normal weight. Remember when I was forced to eat at certain times of day. That was comforting. I did like that. But it doesn't change the fact that I am not hungry. Ok, I will eat around noon. Noon is a good time to eat even if I am not hungry, although yesterday I didn't eat until 2 and I still seemed to eat enough for the day. Well, was it enough for the day? I don't know. I am almost 50 years old now so I don't need to be eating like younger people anymore. I should eat less. I can eat less. I have to be careful, but I should still eat something by noon, but what if Eva wants to get something after she gets off work and I have already eaten so I can't get anything with her. I should just wait until I pick her up and see if she wants to get something, then I can eat after that. That makes sense, I am not even hungry anyway. Yesterday I didn't eat until 2 and let's see, I had a protein bar, wait, I think I had that around 3, right before I picked up Eva. Well, ok so what, it was 3, I just wasn't hungry before 3. There is nothing wrong with not eating when you aren't hungry. Let's see, then I had that salad with avocado dressing, and I even put croutons and avocados and cheese on it. That is a lot of calories, probably 250 plus the protein bar makes 450 and then I had some pork and asparagus and potatoes, but, fuck, the potatoes were like a tablespoon. I did that on purpose, they did look pretty scary, but I did want them, but I had eaten the salad so It's ok to have more asparagus and only a little potatoes. But I did it because I was scared, but also Eva loves the potatoes I make and I wanted her to have them, but also there were a lot of them. 450, 550, 700, 800. 800 calories. Don't forget I had all that chocolate filled with almond butter, it was so good, but I shouldn't have had the rest of it, but it's ok you didn't eat that much for dinner, but it was still a lot, I shouldn't buy that kind anymore, It's too good and I can't control myself around it. 800 calories plus 350, that was probably 350 calories, that is a shit-ton of calories for just chocolate, that is why I can't buy it anymore. Now I am at 1150 and then I had that pineapple. And before bed I had a pear, and a satsuma, that was good, I should get more of those. That must be another 300 calories. 1450... I also had that coffee with cream and oatmilk....and don't forget the sugar...that must be another 300 calories at least. Now I am up to around 1800 calories and I am sure I forgot some things. So 2000. I am sure 2000 calories is plenty for someone my age. I don't need to eat yet. I can wait, I am not hungry, not hungry at all. I didn't eat until 3 yesterday and I still ate plenty. I can wait until 3."

This is my fork in the road. This is my good and evil, my right or wrong. You would think that it would be easy to see the right path when it comes to anorexia recovery, but it isn't. Every moment is met with this constant roll of chatter in my brain. A non stop conversation that is ever present and never shuts up. It goes on and on and on until one direction becomes so foggy and diluted there is only one path left to see. Anorexia's.

Funny Little Liars

Eating disorders are funny little things. They cling to you disguised as guidance, as intelligence, as a best friend. They are always looking out for your best interest, making sure you do the right thing, and make the right choice. And, when you do make the right choice, their right choice, they make you feel so good, so calm, so peaceful. You are gifted with the feeling of invincibility. You are gifted with the feeling of superiority. You are gifted with the feeling of confidence. However, if you dare decide against your eating disorder's sage advice, you will pay dearly. You will be flooded with guilt, rage, fear, and sorrow, the depths of which you didn't know could exist in a human body. You will mourn the choice you should have made, the choice that would have pacified the eating disorder, and these desperate feelings of inadequacy will be so overwhelming you will promise yourself to never deny the eating disorder's voice again. And so you don't.

You follow your eating disorder's words so closely that soon it becomes almost your own voice, indistinguishable from your true self. Now you are just blindly following orders, orders you feel are your own, orders that keep you sane, calm, happy, thin. It becomes harder and harder to untangle the two voices in your head, but here is the thing, the thing you have to hold on to, there are two voices in your head, and one is not you. Even though they are like a chorus singing together now, even though following the eating disorder voice brings peace and even the thought of listening to your true voice brings pain, you have to untangle the two voices, slowly pull them apart, see the lies of the eating disorder weaved within the truth of you. Because eating disorders are such liars.

Take Thanksgiving for example, the entire month before Thanksgiving it will start with its demands and promises.

"Restrict now," it says, "and then you can eat all day on thanksgiving. You can share the holiday with your family, eat freely, and be rewarded for all your hard work restricting now." And so you do.

"Good job," it says, "now just restrict this thanksgiving morning so you can have an amazing guilt free thanksgiving dinner, you are not very hungry anyway, sip some coffee, you will be rewarded with the best dinner." And you do.

"Great work!"

"Wait a minute," it says, "what if you only eat a little dinner now. That would be so smart. Then all of that pre-thanksgiving restricting wouldn't go to waste. Don't ruin it now by eating. You can reward yourself with dessert later if you just stick to a few veggies now." And so you do.

"Oooooh," the eating disorder says, "what a roll you're on, don't eat dessert now, you're doing great, keep the restricting up and maybe you'll even lose a pound this thanksgiving." And so you don't eat, again.

You go to bed hungry and dream of food, you dream of morning crepes with whip cream and berries. You dream of feta and brie and cranberry filled goat's cheese. You dream of turkey doused in gravy. You dream of mashed potatoes and biscuits floating in butter. You eat it all in your dream. This is your true self dreaming, but then your eating disorder wakes you up in a sweaty panic. It makes you search your bed for the remnants of the food that felt so good and real to eat. It makes you grab your stomach to make sure it is empty.

"Wow," the eating disorder shouts ignoring your hunger, "you have basically started a fast this holiday, keep it up, good job," and on and on and on it goes.

Well, the eating disorder is a liar. It keeps promising food later. It keeps promising happiness later. One more missed meal. One more holiday without calories. One more pound to go. It's golden promises are actually lies. One more missed meal really means one more mealtime spent alone, consumed with calculations in my brain. Calculations that the eating disorder uses to drown out my true voice. What a liar. One more holiday without calories really means one more holiday without being present, without my family, without myself. It really means one more holiday in the presence of others, yet completely alone. What a liar. "One more pound to go," it says. One more pound to go? How did I not see this lie a long time ago. One pound is never enough, 10 pounds is never enough, only death would be enough. Lies.

Eating disorders are funny little things. They are stealthy. They are brutal. And, they are liars. This last Thanksgiving my eating disorder told me all of those lies, and more. It kept coming at me. It was mean, it called me names, then it got quiet and calm and tried to speak to me as the voice of reason. It used my voice and made it hard for me to tell it apart from my true self. The battle in my brain was exhausting, but I was done listening to a liar. I ate every day before thanksgiving. I ate all day on thanksgiving, and let me tell you, my eating disorder was screaming. I ate the day after thanksgiving, and I plan to eat everyday, multiple times a day, for the rest of my life, because eating disorders are liars. They are liars and cheaters. They cheat you out of your food. They cheat you out of your family and friends. They cheat you out of your true self. And what do you get in return? Lies.

Mr. Watson

I let go of my scale a year ago. Yes, I am so brave, it was so hard, blah blah blah. The truth is, I miss it, I want it back, without it I am so unsteady. I never quite feel like I am walking on solid ground. Without my scale, without knowing exactly where I stand between gravity and the earth, I am often lost. Every day is a new day in this body. One day I feel certain I am one size, and the next I can gain or lose 5 sizes. It is like my body is a fun house mirror, shifting and changing depending on the angle, the day, the wind. Even my pants are a puzzle, 'were these tight last time?', 'I thought these were my loose pants?', 'Didn't these fit better last time?' Constant confusion.

In truth, I didn't exactly throw my scale away. There was no grand statement as I smashed it with a hammer or ran over it with my car. It simply stopped working. I actually wore out my scale. Everyone with an eating disorder is so different, some count calories, some macros, some nothing. Some weigh, some measure, some do both. There are so many behaviors and idiosyncrasies within each person's disorder, some of these behaviors are mild and nonexistent while others become full blown addictions. Weighing was an absolute addiction for me. I had to do it. Had to. It was like the hit of a drug. I would step on that scale the moment I woke up, every hour if I were home, into the evening, and wake at night to get on it. It was in my dreams. I would do it the same way every time, stepping on three times, moving the scale to a certain spot on the floor each time. The process of weighing myself was numbing. I was possessed and didn't have to feel anything, my body was moving, doing a dance of sorts with the scale, and I was just along for the ride. It was quiet and peaceful, that is until the number showed up. Then my brain was loud again. There was all this cross talk of what the number means, 'it's too big, you gained again fat ass,' or ' it is down, but not enough you dumb bitch, make it lower before you get on next hour.' There was never a peace with the number, it was always abuse that I was too fat or abuse that I was losing too slow, but it was always abuse. Of course, I didn't see it as abuse then, I saw it as the voice of reason. My voice.

At the time that my scale broke I was already into recovery. I was listening to anorexia still, but I was starting to see that perhaps she was not me, just perhaps she did not have my best interests at heart after all. I confessed to my dietitian one day that my scale seemed to be breaking, it was malfunctioning now and then and giving me an error message. I was starting to panic because being in recovery I was now supposed to come to terms with the fact that I should get rid of my scale, but I didn't want to, I wasn't ready, I needed it still. On so many occasions my dietitian would ask me to, tell me to, gently urge me to throw it out. I just could not do it. I could not let it go. Telling her that my scale was dying a slow death seemed to put a motherly smile on her face, and with the kindest eyes she looked straight into me and said, "promise me you will not get a new one, Melissa."

It wasn't long after that my scale died, I honored my promise and did not replace it, but that does not mean the weighing stopped. I would go to the gym to weigh, I would weigh at my mother's house. The thing that did change for me, however, was the feeling I would get while I was weighing. I no longer felt numb, and instead of feeling nothing while doing my dance with the scale, I felt shame. My husband, my dietitian, my teenage girls were all so proud of me for not replacing that scale. Little did they know, I did replace it. I replaced it with the gym scale, my mother's scale, fuck, I even used the walmart scale right in the walmart aisle. I felt like I was cheating on them with the scale. The scale became more important to me than my word. The scale was my mistress, my lover, I would sneak away to be with her. After a few months of cheating with her I had grown weary, exhausted from chasing her around in gyms, stores, and houses. I didn't want her anymore, but I didn't know how to leave her.

Slowly I knew I had to give her up. Recovery is a lot of giving up. Giving up numbers and calculations, giving up controlling my body, giving up, giving up, giving up. It's like we purge one thing after another to make room for a new self to grow. I had to purge the scales, and I had to purge the gym to do that. The gym is an entirely different addiction/behavior that had it's own path to distinguishing, but it was time to let the gym go. Being in recovery, and having a family watch you in recovery, it becomes very difficult to justify the gym. Without the gym, I managed to reduce my love affair with the scale to once a week in my mother's bathroom. It took months for me to slowly wean off of my mother's scale altogether. My strategy was to never use her bathroom. It was an insane strategy I know but the only one I could think of, and it has worked well so far. I have not weighed myself in months now, MONTHS, but I am still anxious about it most days. Take last week for example...

I awoke with all the thoughts of, 'what size even am I', 'Am I growing again or am I the same?', 'I feel huge, wait no I don't, yes I do, no I don't, yes you do you dumbass.' I needed to weigh myself. I told myself I could handle it, whatever the scale said, I could handle it. I was in a better place now. I am doing so good, I am so recovered, so weight restored, so 'healthy', so long has passed, it will give me the information I need to feel more comfortable in my body, blah, blah, blah. My daughter was at my mother's house and I had to pick her up after my 'zoom-therapy'. Perfect, I thought, I will weigh myself at my mother's house later. I will tell them I need to run in and use the bathroom, I will wear shoes that are easy to slip off, and just like that, I will be on and off that scale and then I will feel so much better. I felt like I was planning a rendezvous with a lover, and in truth I was, I was in love with scale, I missed it, I wanted it.

Then I mentioned to my therapist that I had the intention of weighing myself. I cannot explain why I mentioned it to her, except that perhaps it is a sign my real self was trying to save me from anorexia creeping back in to lure me away. She ever so gently pondered with me until I realized for myself I would not be meeting my lover today. We talked about why my brain runs to anorexia, and knowing that there is an evolutionary reason for my suffering creates a scaffold from which I can climb out of the anorexic thinking and back into my real brain. Yes I was sad I wouldn't be weighing today, I was somber and my body shook as I picked up my daughter too afraid to even go in mother's house.

Later that night I would get the real reward for not giving in to anorexia. My sweet husband came home from work and surprised me with a night to ourselves in a hotel. I was sitting in this hotel, wrapped in nothing but a sheet, eating breaded and fried cauliflower, pita bread with a myriad of sauces, and fries, lots of fries, with my husband across from me. I stopped for a moment and took in the peace that I felt. I was naked. I was eating. I was happy. It was something I thought would never happen, especially at my current size that I never thought I would feel comfortable at. But I did feel comfortable. I did feel OK with my body. I realized right in that moment that if I had given in and weighed myself earlier everything would be different. I would be consumed by the number on the scale, thinking about losing pounds instead of laughing at losing the ketchup packet in the sheets. I would be worried about every calorie, and just have coffee, instead of sharing in lemon cake and tiramisu.

I am loads bigger today than when I was secretly having an affair with the scale. I never thought I could be happy here. But the thing is, I am. My husband loves my body this size. My children love a mother they can hug and not be afraid of when all they feel is bones. Most importantly though, for all of us with this same love affair, is that our life is so much better without our mistress in it. She was stealing away our food, our time, and our happiness. It is time we take it back, and it starts by breaking up with her for good. She won't change how we feel when we look in the mirror and see our bodies morph and change. Stepping on that scale just gives more power to the dysmorphia and the pathway you have built for anorexia to sneak back in and grow in power.

Someday, much like an ex-lover you see in a coffee shop after years have gone by, I will be able to get on a scale and say, 'oh, there you are, it's been a while,' but today is not that day, today the scale is still connected to anorexia, and thankfully I did not run back to her, but instead I ran to my husband and my real life. And I truly believe because I made the right choice I was gifted, gifted with the hotel, gifted with a body I wasn't ashamed of, and gifted with cake, and fries, and chocolates, and on, and on. The gifts are different for all of us but I truly believe they are waiting, we just have to give up anorexia to get them.

All the Foods

Waking up today I had an overwhelming urge to make Christmas cookies. It has been years. But I am better now. I can eat almost all the foods. I can fight almost all the urges. I am ready to bake again, and by bake again, I mean bake and enjoy the food with my family. As I lay here in my bed I think of the things I want to make, gingerbread and sugar cookies. It has been more than a decade since I have spent the day in my kitchen, enjoying the smells, tasting the doughs. I started to get excited, thinking of all the Christmas sweets I have missed out on over the years.

I crawled out of bed looking forward to my day, slowly showered and dressed, all the while sipping my coffee. I landed in my kitchen and took out my big glass dough bowl. I took a minute to look around. I have missed this. The cool spanish tiles under my feet. The faint noise of CNN coming from the other room. I top off my coffee for the third time and start measuring flour, the dough needs to get into the refrigerator soon so it has time to cool before I can roll it this afternoon. I start with the gingerbread as I am hungry for the smells of molasses and spice. The strong scent that rises as I grate the nutmeg reminds me I have yet to eat this morning.

"That's OK, I can put off eating until I make this dough, after all it needs to get into the fridge, I am not even hungry yet anyway. I am healed. I can eat whenever I want now. Just to show anorexia she has no control over me I think I will have a piece of mom's fruitcake with my breakfast. Mmmm....yes...fruitcake sounds so good...."

I separate my giant batch of gingerbread into five disks, wrap them, and pop them in the fridge. I look at the clock, between keeping up on the laundry and getting the dough made it is almost noon, but I also have to get the sugar cookie dough in the fridge so it can chill. I ponder eating. I am still sipping on coffee, and I am still not hungry. I should follow my hunger, right? Intuitive eating, right? I decide to make my next dough and then sit with a nice meal. I turn on some classic Christmas music and get lost in washing these dishes and making my next dough. As I slip the sugar dough upon the gingerbread and close the door to the refrigerator I turn around to see it is after one o'clock already.

"Oh wow, I guess I should eat. Normal people would eat by now. But I am not even hungry and normal people don't eat if they aren't hungry. I know, I know, I am not a normal person, I have anorexia, but also I am doing so good. I am beating this. I shouldn't eat a big meal if I am not hungry. Right? Normal people follow their intuition, their hunger cues. What do I want to eat? I know what I will have. I will sit down and have a cup of tea with a nice slice of fruitcake. That sounds so fancy, so comforting, so Christmas like. I don't need a full meal, there is so many calories in fruitcake anyway it is like having a full meal. I mean, it can't be an eating disorder choice if I am gobbling down fruitcake....right?"

I slowly cut a slice of fruitcake, realize it is too thick and cut it in half. I put the half slice on a plate and set it on the table next to a cup of tea. It crosses my mind to have a piece of fruit with it, perhaps a sliced apple or a few clementines, but then fruitcake already has fruit and nuts in it so why bother. I triumphantly eat my fruitcake until the plate lies empty even of crumbs and then finish off my tea, thinking about how far I have come in my recovery. I think about last year when I could not bear to even taste the fruitcake for fear it would start a binge. I think of how nice it just felt to sit down at my table and enjoy a piece this year. After setting my plate in the sink I open the fridge and poke a finger at the dough sitting on the bottom of the stack to see how stiff it has gotten. It's getting close, perhaps another hour. Then I notice a small milk spill on the refrigerator shelf below the dough so I grab my cleaner and towel...which leads to seeing leftovers that needed to be thrown away....which leads to the entire refrigerator getting emptied and cleaned....right down to the veggie drawers.

Christmas music on, family walking in and out, scrubbing the walls of the fridge, this is my happy place, this is my safety, this is my calm. I retreat into the cleaning, into the numbness. My family is near creating a safe bubble, but in reality I am alone in my head without thoughts. I like it here and so I stay awhile. Hours pass. Eventually, I finish with the scrubbing and it is time to start the cookies baking. The clock shows after four and food crosses my mind for the first time since the fruitcake.

"Shoot, shoot, shoot, it's after four, I should grab more food to eat. Normal people would eat lunch by now. I know, I'll just start the cookies baking and then grab something. Wait, I am for sure going to want some of the cookies I bake, I mean, I am practically recovered now, and that is what normal people do, right? Normal people eat the cookies they bake, they eat them warm out of the oven and they enjoy them. That's what I will do, I will have my own cookies right from the oven! What a treat! I sure could not have done this last year!"

Cookies get rolled, cut, and baked. They cool. They stack. They get rolled, cut, and baked some more. There doesn't seem to be time for me to grab a few and eat them, although I do find time to put all the broken ones in a bowl and give them to my husband. As the last batch cools on the racks, and after I finish washing the cookie sheets, I make myself a sweet and milky chai tea. I sit at the table and pick the best one to eat myself. Again, as I eat my perfectly shaped gingerbread man I can't help but feel triumphant. I am winning at recovery. I am eating the treats. I am sharing in the holiday! This moment is what recovery is for. A brief thought crosses my mind that I should eat something else but a cookie has a lot of calories and now that I make chai sweet and with real half and half it seems so unnecessary to add more food to this snack. There is carbs, protein, fats, and lots of calories, it might as well be a meal.

My husband walks in with his empty bowl from his broken cookie pieces and wonders aloud about dinner. Dinner. I forgot all about dinner, I was so busy with my baking and cleaning. I don't feel like eating dinner anyway as I just finished my meal of the largest gingerbread cookie and a sweet milky tea so thick it might as well have been soup. I offer to heat up some leftovers, then inform him that I am too full to eat dinner myself because of my triumphant sweets eating, and besides, I need to get the frosting and sprinkles ready for the cookies.

It is getting late into the evening as I start frosting. My 17 and 20 year old daughters are actually in the house and so I cajole them into the kitchen to help me frost. They complain at first but before you know it even my husband starts frosting some cookies. The four of us sit frosting, and sprinkling, and laughing for a few hours. I feel so strong in my recovery. I am so sure anorexia is in the past that I pick up a frosted cookie and eat it on the spot with my family. It feels freeing. It feels accomplished. I could not be scarfing frosted Christmas cookies on a whim if I were still deep in anorexia, right?

My husband wanders off eventually and my girls leave to their phones in the other rooms. I finish packing up the cookies and can't stop thinking about how great it is that I can share in the holiday sweets like everyone else. I can eat fruitcake and cookies and drink milky chai's. I slice myself an apple to snack on before going to bed for the night and as I fall asleep I think to myself that tomorrow I am going to bake again. I am finally doing it. I am baking. I am eating what I bake. I am recovered.

The next day I make fudge, I make rainbow cookies, and I eat them. Fudge has a lot of fat and carbs so it might as well be a meal in and of itself, and if you add soupy thick chai tea to rainbow cookies I think that is more than enough food to be a meal as well. The day after that I make cranberry breads and sandwich cookies. Again, no one would argue that bread is a breakfast food and sandwich cookies, well, sandwich is in the name so lunch it shall be. I could not be happier this year that I am actually taking part in eating all of the holiday foods. I can bake again. I can eat the sweets like everyone else.

As I am standing at the counter frosting and pushing the sandwich cookies together I notice the avocados are bad. They were ripe when I bought them some days ago and I was looking forward to having them in a sandwich or chopped on a bowl of warm corn. That is when I saw anorexia. She was staring at me from the rotten avocados. She had been with me for days and I didn't even notice her arrival. She arrived with my fruitcake. She let me have fruitcake, she even let me feel happy and triumphant over the fruitcake. She let me have gingerbread, and fudge, and milky tea. But what she didn't let me have was anything else. The fruitcake was my breakfast. The warm gingerbread was my lunch. The frosted cookie I was so proud of, it was my dinner. And the apple was my dessert. That is all she let me eat the day she arrived. She told me I didn't need more. She told me the sweets had enough fats and calories that they were my meals, and I listened. I believed her. For three days she told me this until the avocado broke her spell and I could see her. But, even though I could see her again, I still believed her words. She made sense after all, there was a lot of calories in these treats. I had to compensate somewhere. How could I eat all of the treats and also regular food. Surely that is too much food. She made perfect sense to me as she spoke. I could make no arguments. I could not disagree.

So I reached out. I was confused. I knew I was supposed to eat but anorexia was making too much sense to disobey. I needed another opinion. I sent an email to my dietician, I am sure I sounded like a rambling fool. Going on and on about eating too many sweets, but I am supposed to eat sweets, but then how do I eat other food, I am supposed to eat other food, but that is too many calories, too much food, it seems wrong to eat so much, so do I just eat regular food and no sweets, do people actually eat this much food, I think I am doing this eating thing all wrong, I can't figure it out, can Christmas just end already, it is all just too much to figure out, I shouldn't have eaten the fruitcake in the first place, and on and on.

"Melissa, It is normal to eat the treats. It is normal to eat the treats in addition to your regular food. Please remember that there are certain celebratory times of year where it is normal to enjoy the things that go along with the season. It is special and temporary. Most people don't take away something in order to appreciate something seasonal. It is understandable that anorexia would try to take advantage of that! It is a holiday. The treats do not need to be made up for. If it is summer and the apricots are ripe you eat a lot of extra apricots, but you also eat your regular foods. If it is someone's birthday you will eat cake, but you also eat your regular foods. If you bake fresh cookies you eat a lot of warm cookies from the oven, but you also eat your regular foods. Your body works it out. Your body knows what to do with the food. Your body is not a calculator and at Christmas time you eat the treats and you eat your regular foods. Eat the treats. Eat your regular foods. It is normal. It is safe."

Anorexia was wrong. Fruitcake is not breakfast. Gingerbread is not lunch. Sugar cookies are not dinner. In my haste to run toward intuitive eating and listen to my hunger I fell into anorexia's arms again. She was seductive and clever the way she lured me in with false feelings of triumph and calm. She sounded so clear disguised as my own voice, leading me right down the path she wanted me to take. I won't lie, her path did feel good, it felt right, it felt calm. It felt like an old friend ready to wrap me up in a warm blanket. But seeing that avocado reminded me of my other path, my recovery path, and that path feels like authenticity, fresh air, and light. It feels like the unconditional love I can finally give my family because it isn't all tied up in her games. It feels like conversations with my girls or warm embraces with my husband. My recovery path, even though it may be long, It feels like life. And life, well, real life, it has ALL the foods.

Part 3
Holding On

Misguided Angel

Anorexia came back this morning and I woke with her heavy on my chest. I laid in bed for a few minutes trying to shake her off, but she just bore down harder with the weight of sadness and loss. I sat up feeling fog roll into my head and realized I have no reason to rise, no purpose to start the day. Without her in my life I have no miles to run, calories to count, or even a scale to weigh myself on. I am alone.

I sit here and wonder what is left of me. Anorexia was my best friend, my spouse, my mother. She was my confidant, my safe place, and my medication. She was all I needed, but she was also killing me, and because I wouldn't leave my children I was forced to fight back. I began to nail her in her coffin. I gained weight against her voice that kept telling me to shrink. I sat still when she yelled at me to run. I cried on the bathroom floor feeling my food digest instead of watching it flush away. I was closing her in one nail at a time.

Until this morning. She came back not with the usual thoughts of 'don't eat' or 'you are fat'. No, this morning she came back to remind me that I am nothing without her. She is my everything, she takes care of me, she gives focus and meaning to every moment. I sat in bed listening to her and I realized she is right, she is an angel, my angel. She came to me from my ancestors, always in my blood, in my brain, ready to save me from famine and lead me to the promise land. From the moment she awoke in me she gave me all the tools I needed, restriction to feel calm and focused, exercise to feel strong and powerful. Most importantly, she took my mind at a time that it needed taking. She filled my days with calculations so I couldn't think of the family that stole my innocence. She had me running in circles to numb the pain when my daughter tried to die. She saved my life time and time again by taking away my feelings because she knew I wasn't ready for them.

When I started fighting her I also started feeling again. As I gained weight I had to remember the pain of my childhood and I had to feel it for the first time. I felt such sadness for that little girl. As I sat with food I also sat with the sorrow of watching my own little girl not wanting to be in this world anymore. Without Anorexia's protection I could now feel her pain and it was excruciating. For years I would try to leave Anorexia, only to feel too much pain, and run back again. After all, she was helping me, keeping me from the pain, keeping my mind occupied. Anorexia was always there to make sure I was safe, alive. The thing is, while she was trying her best to save me, to save me from famine, to save me from feeling, to save me from myself, she was also so misguided. She was keeping me from feeling love. She was keeping me from being a wife, a mother, from sharing emotions with the people I love. She was keeping me from living. Her attempt to save me was killing me. I kept fighting.

So she came to me again this morning to remind me of how long the days are without her. To remind me how much easier it is not to feel. She wanted to let me know that I need her more than I need my own breath. She reminded me of how much I miss her, and she is right, I miss her. She stayed with me all morning, an angel on my shoulder, trying to lead me down the right path, her path. I tried to ignore her, I flirted with her, I imagined running back to her. I tried running away from her, then I cried over her, until finally, all that was left was to call her by name.

I got in my car and drove. I put on her playlist, songs just for her, our songs.

"I hear you. Yes, I agree, I miss you, more than you know. More than anyone knows. I miss you to the point of pain, of tears."

She is right, my days are long without her. She is right that she would save my life if I were in a famine. She is right that she makes me feel so good. But, mixed into all this right, she is also misguided. My long days are long because I have yet to learn to live with myself on my own without her. The famine in my brain is not real and I will die running from it. And, yes, she makes me feel so good because much like an abusive husband she cut me off from everyone else so all of my emotions were tied to her and how well I obeyed her.

I drove in my car and I mourned her, even though she was right there with me. I talked to her, I played music with her, I cried with her. Then, I changed the song. I wiped my eyes and played music that I could feel, that I could sing to, and I drove home. Anorexia's songs will always be on my playlist, I will not pretend they aren't there or run away. There is one nail in her coffin not quite nailed down, at least for now, and that is OK. When she needs to talk to me I will listen to her, cry with her, miss her. But then I have to move on, start my real day, with my real family, not with my misguided angel.

I walked back in my home, past my teenager on the couch, smiling because I can now feel so much love and empathy for her. I found my husband and let him hold me and my swollen eyes, he didn't ask why, he just held me. Then I went into the kitchen and opened the fridge, because misguided angel on my shoulder or not, I eat.

WTF is all this night eating?

This question has haunted me for decades. I am a night eater. Always have been. I love the peace and silence of eating with the night. All day I look forward to that time after dinner, after the chores are done, after kids are in bed, when I can sit with myself and enjoy a hard earned treat, or two, or three. I can set down my anxiety and just be with the food, taking in the sensations of textures and tastes. I can have salty and cheesy or doughy and sweet, or both. I work hard all day, I try to be kind, give my all to friends and family, fulfilling all their needs, waiting to give to myself until the evening. So when the evening comes, and it is my turn, I need it, I deserve it, I can't live without it. My night eating is my comfort, my gift to myself for surviving another day being me, surviving the day being filled with anxiety and having walls so high it takes the smooth taste of chocolate in a dim kitchen to begin to lower them. With every sweet and salty bite my walls begin to lower and I just feel good, I just feel me, I just feel nothing.

The thing about night eating, though, is that it never stayed the same, it was always morphing and changing. Sometimes my few treats after dinner would turn into second meals such as grilled cheese or frozen TV dinners, always followed still by a few more treats. Sometimes I would skip dinner and get right to my after dinner treats. I was never much of a breakfast eater but at this point I began to fear breakfast. By the morning I was still full of guilt from the night eating so I stopped eating breakfast altogether and often skipped lunch as well to make up for the evening before. My little evening treat to myself had now taken on a life of its own and I could not stop doing it.

This morphed again and along with the after dinner meals I was waking in the night to eat. I would wake up from sleep and my first thought would be "what is in the kitchen, what can I eat." I would wander, fully aware of myself, into the kitchen and have a snack. I would sit with the open ice cream container and tub of peanut butter slipping my spoon into both. I would sneak some cookies from my husbands 'snack' cupboard or some sweets from the sweet bin. Then I could go back to sleep. There were times I would get up in the middle of the night and sit on the toilet to pee and my brain would fight within itself. I would try to convince my brain I didn't need to go eat again in the kitchen....but my brain would always tell me I can't go back to sleep without a snack, I can't, my body won't allow it....and I already knew my brain was right so I would hurry in for a quick snack so I could go back to bed, only to do it again a few hours later.

Along with the constant night eating came a loss of daytime appetite. The mere sight or smell of food in the morning made me sick. Of course this could be because only a few hours earlier, in the darkness of predawn, I had probably eaten another snack. Surprisingly this aversion to food during the day felt so good to me, it felt powerful, it made me feel like I was better than other people because I didn't need food all day like they did. I felt like I had an edge up during the day, and with my mile high walls of anxiety I was carrying around with me, it was an intoxicating feeling. It calmed my feelings of inadequacy because it gave me a superpower, the superpower of restriction.

Then anorexia hit hard. I had a functional eating disorder my entire life, never getting underweight enough to be noticed as sick. My eating disorder was disguised as dieting, I would cut out all fat until my skin was so dry it would crack, I would try every cleanse or fat reducing pill on the market, I would cycle through restrict-binge-purge cycles regularly, but I never earned the title of anorexic because my weight never plummeted. That is, until the night eating showed up and took away my daytime hunger. Without daytime hunger I could endlessly restrict myself to eating only after dinner. Soon my one meal of dinner was a bowl of spinach and my night eating was my only real intake. Night eating persisted all through my sickest days with anorexia, but eventually, and many years later, I was drawn to recover.

This is when night eating became my savior. Night eating literally saved my life. This thing that I hated so much, that I couldn't get rid of, that I am a slave to, saved my life. When my brain was overtaken by my ancestors forcing me to flee a famine I couldn't see it was the night eating that saved my life. It was the night eating that kept me alive. Some biological safety mechanism in my brain forced food down my throat at 2 am. And 3 am. And sometimes 4 am. In the depths of my sickest days with anorexia I was so angry with my night eating. It was in the way of the next pound I needed to lose. I had control over everything I put in my mouth, until the middle of the night, and anorexia was pissed, but even anorexia couldn't beat the night eating, and so it persisted.

My anorexia turned me to bones and I was forced to battle it. For over two years I battled, little win after little win, I moved slowly through recovery. I fought the ancient evolutionary voices in my head, all the while my night eating continued. In the beginning of recovery when eating was so hard I tried to embrace the night eating as a gift that could help me get more calories in. I needed the extra nourishment and if it came at 2 am I was happy for that. I gained to my set point, perhaps with some overshoot, and anorexia had quieted to a tolerable level.

But, the night eating is still here. "I prefer to eat late," I tell myself. "I was never a morning eater," I tell myself. "I eat all my meals, they are just shifted later," I tell myself. All of these things are true. But also, it is true I hate night eating. It is time to let it go, and the only way to let it go is to get rid of the last and most ingrained part of my eating disorder, morning anorexia.

Morning anorexia is common in most with night eating. It makes sense. Why would I be hungry in the morning when I had eaten so late or in the middle of the night. There is also some truth in the fact that I have shifted my circadian pattern of food intake. Likely it took time for me to shift this pattern in the wrong direction, so it stands to reason it will take me a while to shift it back. It is also very scary to eat in the morning after consuming high calorie snacks late at night. But also, shifting all of your food times earlier is imperative to overcoming this, you have to do it. The tricky part becomes when the night eating and morning eating have to happen at the same time, but they will have to, at least for a while. There will be a time you force feed yourself breakfast after eating just a few hours earlier alone in the dark kitchen. There is no skipping this part, there is no way around it. It will feel wrong and your brain will be screaming at you not to do it, but you have to, you have to eat the food. Eat when you wake up, eat a few hours later, eat a few hours after that. You are retraining your brain and body when it's feeding times are. If it is still hungry in the middle of the night, great, eat then too....but never skip the mornings.

Do I think I have a cure for night eating? Definitely not. It is the hardest thing I have ever fought. It makes me mad. It makes me sad. It makes me feel worthless and hopeless some nights. Do I think there is a way out? Most definitely, YOU HAVE TO EAT IN THE MORNING. But it sucks, and it's hard, and it is like I am letting go of a best friend. A best friend that was always there for me in the night, that listens to my worries, that drowns my fears in chocolate. But it is time that I depend on the real people in my life for comfort, love, and acceptance, and if they are not available then it is time I learn to depend on someone who always is....myself.

Where We Met

I drove by our meeting place today. I had to slow to catch my breath as I could feel you calling me in. I wanted to pull into our favorite parking spot and sit with the feel of you for a while, it has been so long. When you were in my life everything seemed so simple. There was one goal, one plan, one you. All I had to do was focus on you and all the other stressors of my life would fade into the backdrop, like the blur of traffic driving by as I sat alone with you, in my car, in our spot. I wish we could have just one more rendezvous, one more moment of peace and solitude and complete numbness. Just one more. I couldn't help myself and I pulled over to the side of the road, too afraid to pull into our spot. I parked where I could see it, close enough that I could feel it. I watched for a while, our empty spot, thinking just one more time can't hurt. I just need that time with you again, that sweet, sweet time right after. Those moments that fill my head with both ecstasy and numbness. That time that steadies my nerves and calms my brain for hours. Oh, how I want it, need it, love it.

I thought of one of the times we met, or was it all of the times we met?

***

It was in the afternoon. I had been planning to meet you since the day before, I dreamt of you throughout the night, I mapped out my path to you in my head. I woke in the morning tasting you on my lips, excited for the salt, the sugar and the fat, oh all the fat.

I left work to start my route to see you, it always started the same. The grocery store. I started in the bakery section, looking over the pastries, cakes, and donuts. We had donuts at work yesterday and I wanted one so badly that I promised to get myself one today. I got a chocolate one, a maple one, a twisted one, and a glazed one. I plopped them in the top of the cart making a mental note to not shift the bag too much and scrape off any icing. Then come the cookies, giant chocolate chip cookies, and the cake, a slice of chocolate and a slice of vanilla. Cheesecake slices are next, and then I find the individually wrapped bars and sweets. I pick a few out but as I put them in the cart I look in and realize it is too much food, more than I can eat, but I can't put any back, I have to taste it all. I have the thought that this is crazy, I am crazy, but also, I have no choice but to go with the crazy. I have to satisfy all of my cravings at once or else meeting you will be all for naught. I go toward the deli as if on auto pilot. I ask for a corndog, some mac and cheese, some sort of pizza roll, and a chicken strip. I turn from the deli and see the frozen food section. Ice cream. I love ice cream, but I can't eat ice cream, Anorexia forbids it. Here is the wonderful thing about meeting you, though, I can eat all the things. I can eat the ice cream. I can eat anything. You don't judge me, you accept me, you encourage me, you make me feel so so good.

So I go right down that aisle and get Ben and Jerry's Ice cream. I tell myself to just get one pint because It is a waste of money to get two, but I can't decide between flavors so I throw both pints in the cart anyway. I come out the other side of the frozen section and turn to make my way to the snacks.

I head right for the candy and grab anything with peanut butter. Peanut butter Twix, peanut butter Snickers, multiple types of Reese's all get thrown in. I have one last stop to make before the register. I move into the next aisle and look at the bottled water. I need the large size bottles. I always keep bottles of water hidden under my car seat, but I am always worried it won't be enough. I need more. Some bottled water has electrolytes now and I am tempted to try those but then I worry it will throw my levels off even worse if I lose electrolytes and then put them back in so quickly just to lose them again a second time. I stick with three extra tall bottles of regular water. I am always nervous at the checkout counter. I am scared I will know the checker, I am scared I will know another customer in line, I am scared of the judgment, I am scared they will look at what I am buying and know who I am meeting. I am just scared. I quickly put my food on the belt, make some lame joke about feeding teenagers, and get out of there. Out of there and back to the safety of my car.

I put all my bags in the passenger seat, careful to find the donuts and place them gingerly on the top. I still have a few more stops to make before we can meet. I need the taco place, and not just tacos. I need a burrito, a soft taco, a quesadilla, potatoes smothered in cheese, sour cream, and guacamole, and a large diet coke with no ice. The car starts smelling so good, all the bakery smells mixed with the fried food smells, I can hardly wait. The only thing that keeps me from sneaking into the bags is time. I only have so much time once I start eating. If I eat too soon I am afraid some of the food will absorb into my body. That thought terrifies me every time I come to meet you, yet I still come, I cannot control myself, you are my addiction. I continue on to Mcdonalds. My kids ate Mcdonalds the other day and I need to eat everything I watched them eat, and more. I ordered a big mac with extra sauce, a McChicken, pancakes with syrup, a McGriddle, fries, an oreo Mcflurry with extra oreo, and a large diet coke with no ice. I pray as I pull up that the person in the window is not a school friend of one of my daughters. As I pull away the fear subsides and is replaced with sweet calm. Suddenly everything is ok. Everything is at peace and I know now that for the next hour it will just be me and you. I am a mix of excitement and numb as I reach into the bag and pull out some fries. The taste is indescribable. After that first bite my entire body lets out a huge sigh and I sink a little more into my seat as I drive to our spot. On the way I toggle between bites of oreo Mcflurry, fries, and huge gulps of diet coke.

I pull into our spot and turn off the engine. I pop the trunk and jump out to retrieve the bag I have hidden amongst the larger bags of auto supplies meant for emergencies. I jump back in the car, push my front seat back to give myself more room, slip off my shoes, and turn to look at all the food. I set the trunk bag in the backseat and organize all of my cravings on the passenger seat, throwing the water bottles into the back. I eat. I taste big mac, I taste oreo, I think I even taste chocolate, but then the tasting ends and the needing begins. I need some of this and then I need some of that. I need the McDonald's food so that next time my kids have it it won't sting so bad. I need to eat the cookies so when my husband eats his in front of me I can remind myself to stay strong and starve. I can have cookies too, just not with him, I can have them in my car, in my car with you. I need to have some Ben and Jerry's because I love ice cream and it is now or never. So I eat more. I am full almost immediately but I keep going. I eat most of the big mac, some quesadilla, half of each donut, a cookie dipped in ice cream, bites of this, and pieces of that. I gulp down diet coke in between every few bites, lots and lots of diet coke. I finish one diet coke and start on the other. I don't taste. I just eat.

After both diet cokes are gone and my stomach feels so full it may explode I start combining packages and bags. I smash all the fast food bags into grocery bags and tie knots in the tops of each bag. Then I make my way into the back seat and grab a bottle of water. I chug it as I reach into my trunk bag and pull out my plastic tub. It took me a while to find the perfect sized plastic tub to use and this one is just that. A large deep gallon ice cream bucket. Next, I reach in and pull out a giant ball of plastic grocery store bags. I open one up. I open another up and put it inside the first, I repeat the process until I have four layers of grocery bags. Then I line the plastic bucket with the bags. This process is like the lighting of a cigarette, the chopping of a line, wrapping the rubber around your arm. It is anticipation. It is like the knowing you have before orgasm, or the last moments before you lose consciousness. I reach into the pocket behind the driver's seat and pull out my window shades, opening one in each side window. The feeling of aloneness overtakes me but I like it. I pull the towel from under the passenger's seat and lay it across my lap as I spread my legs wide, one behind each seat.

It always takes me a moment to start. My hair is up, my towel is on, my bucket is lined. I lean over my bowl and just stare in for a moment. I feel like I am procrastinating but also I begin to panic because I have to get the food out of me.

Time is ticking and I can feel it start to digest. I shove my fingers down my throat and I am so full of food that it flies up out of me without warning, but I am prepared. It flies into the bucket seemingly without end and I start to lose my breath. Even though I am panting when the vomiting pauses my fingers go right back in. More comes out. Over and over until my lips and hands are held together by strings of drool. I can hardly take a breath but this is the time. This is what I came for.

Everything stops. I am leaning over the bowl but I don't see vomit. I don't see. I just feel my breath starting to slow and I feel a calmness and clarity that I feel nowhere else in my life. Not with my job, not in my home, not with my husband or my kids. It feels like heaven. It feels like nothing and no one else exists. I don't need anyone. I don't need anything. I don't need food. I am perfectly calm now but I am still not done. I have to finish. I have to get any remnants of food left, so I drink the last two bottles of water as fast as I can and I throw my fingers down my throat again. I keep going until my fingers are coated in yellowish bile and my throat tastes the sour of my stomach juices. That is when I know I am done. I wipe up with Mcdonald's napkins and tie the vomit bag into triple knots. I set the vomit on the floor and pause. I take in the good feelings. The feelings of being fed, of being satisfied, of being numb, of simply being. Time is now a combination of good feelings and a lack of feelings all at the same time. How can I not chase this? How can I not come back for more? Time passes and I sit with you.

As if the world is in slow motion, I put the car shades away, climb into the front seat and look into the visor mirror. My eyes are black from mascara and it looks like I have been crying. I open the glove box and pull out my makeup bag and fix myself up. I grab the vomit bags out of the bucket, and the trash, including all of the uneaten food, and toss it into the dumpster across the street behind me. I get back into the car and just sit there feeling good, feeling calm, feeling nothing. I put the makeup bag away and pull out my bottle of tums and toss a few in my mouth to chew on the way home. I spray perfume and always keep the windows down to air out the smell of you. Then, just like that, it is over. It is over but I am left with the good feelings. The world is still in slow motion. I don't want food, I don't need food, I don't need anything, at least for a while, for hours even. For hours I am in the clouds.

***

The thing is, though, while sitting on the side of the road, as I was remembering meeting you that afternoon, my mind also remembered other things. I remembered how you kept wanting more and more and more. You were never satisfied. You took over my thoughts, my life. We started by meeting every other week, sometimes once a month. It was a nice getaway from my life, a safety net for my restriction. You were there when I needed you and I looked forward to sneaking away to see you. I didn't feel too guilty, I could justify you as just a 'weak moment' now and then. Then, I found myself slipping out to see you weekly. I promised myself that weekly would be enough, weekly could satisfy me, cure my cravings. It didn't. I blinked and weekly turned into every day. Before I could even try and protest, every day turned into twice a day.

You became all I could think about. My life revolved around thinking about meeting you, planning to meet you, secretly meeting you, hiding that I met you. I was buying food for us. So. Much. Food. Food I ate. Food I didn't eat. Food I wasted both by throwing it away or throwing it up. I was hiding food in my car, in my house, in my purse. I was always hiding. All for those few moments, few hours, of peace and calm. But, even those few hours got shorter and shorter. Soon, as quickly as I would leave you I would find myself thinking of when I could see you again. You weren't satisfied. I wasn't satisfied. We were like two lost souls trying to feel better in each other's arms, but all we felt after those first few moments of relief was guilt and shame. Guilt over needing to eat at all. If I were good I wouldn't need to binge like this. If I just had enough willpower I could stop and go back to just restricting. Guilt over wasting food, wasting money, wasting time, all that time. The shame was unparalleled by any I have felt before. Shame over such a disgusting act. My face in a bucket of vomit with drooly slime running down my chin, my arms, spilling off my elbow. My nose filled with gunk so that I can't breathe but I am unwilling to pause because getting all the food out comes before breathing. The splash in my face, the feeling of it hitting my hair, and the smell. I smell you in my nose all day and night, and the shame of you floods back with each whiff. The shameful panic I feel knowing I can't wash you out, there is never enough soap, you are always there to remind me that I am unworthy, weak, and unlovable.

Then there is the shame that comes with being unworthy, weak, and unlovable. I am a wife. I am a mom. I should not be meeting you in a parking lot. I should not be cleaning you off my car seats like a man cleaning lipstick off his collar. I should not be hiding food receipts like one hides hotel receipts from an affair. But I do hide. I hide the receipts. I hide vomit stains. I mask the smell of you with perfumes and lotions. I hide plastic bags and buckets in my trunk. And I try to hide my shame. But shame lies on me day and night like a shroud. The shame is palpable, both to me and my family, even if they don't exactly know why. I know why. It is from meeting you. It is from this game that is no longer a game I play with you. It is from secrets. Shame is woven with secrets, and the fabric I have woven is thick.

I remember the first time you hurt me, caused me pain, caused me to bleed. I lived in fear day and night. I vowed to stop. I didn't. I prayed for you to leave me as I didn't have the strength to leave you. You didn't. I was so afraid, afraid of ripping myself open, afraid of loosing teeth, afraid of doctors, afraid of being found out, afraid of you, but still I came running back. I always ran back.

Until I didn't. It was hard and it was slow. First, I stood you up one day, it was sheer terror. I sat home rocking back and forth alone, white knuckles, tears, anger. I stood you up again and you realized I was trying to leave you. You grabbed on tighter, reminding me of how much I need you, and I did need you, but I also needed my family and I realized you were smothering them out of my life. I was putting you before them. I was seeing you before them. I was loving you more than them. I would stand you up, then I would run to you, then I would run away from you, then I would run back to you. Finally, I started to get smart. I started to play your game. When I would see an opening in my schedule and start to think of meeting you I would act. I would try not to think too much and instead grab for my phone. I would text my daughter, my other daughter, my husband, even my mother. I would ask them out for a snack, a coffee, a meal. And it worked. Inevitably one of them would accept my invitation and instead of sneaking off to see you I would spend my time with them, my real loves, my real family. Of course as I was sitting with them I was always thinking of you, I was calculating calories and worried about gaining. I was missing your release, your moments of sheer ecstasy. I know how intoxicating you are, especially after eating, so I always made sure I stayed with someone for the rest of the day. I failed sometimes. Some months more than others. But I didn't stop trying to escape you.

I cried over you for months. Then I cried over you less. One day I realized I forgot to think about you. I forgot you existed. I was sad. I was sad I forgot about you because you were my everything. You were my confidant, my best friend, my drug. You solved all my problems and made me feel so so good. Perhaps that is why I look back on you so fondly? Isn't that what the human brain is wired to do? Remember the good times, gloss over the bad? I looked back at you today as I was parked on the side of the road with rose colored glasses on. It is only when I truly stopped to remember you that I remembered all the underpinnings of your abuse. You gave me a false sense of security so you could try to steal my life away and it almost worked. You gave me calm. You gave me peace. You gave me anticipation and then ecstasy. But much like plucking a rose, you can't forget to watch for the thorns. The pain, the addiction, the way you keep me away from those I love. Yes, I can drive by, and yes, I can feel the good feelings, but then I need to pull over and truly remember, because if I am going to let myself remember you, I have to remember ALL of you. So, now when I drive by our spot and see the place we met, at first I may see only the roses, but if I stop and look hard enough, the thorns always expose themselves, too.

Part 4
The Cliche Of Freedom

Cheating Again?

I have been cheating again. Like a mistress in the dark, I meet your voice and invite you in.

"How have you been?" I should not speak to you but cannot help myself, "I have missed you so."

'I have been alone and waiting...and you?'

"How am I? Not good, I have been catching glimpses of you in mirrors and empty plates, everywhere really. I have been running and running until my breath is lost and still you are there, ahead of me even, as if you know where I will run next."

'But I do know where you will run, and I will always be around the next turn, waiting... and I am safe, that is why I am always there, I am safe and I am calm and I will be there waiting whenever you are ready to return.'

"But, I told you, I will never return, I have already mourned and cried until my tears ran out of wetness and all that was left was the salty crust of anger. Anger because you stole so much from me. You stole so much yet I still mourn you and want you back."

'I am still here.'

"Yes you are, little reminders of you everywhere. It is sad. It is terrifying. It is love."

'Then come back.'

"You make it sound so easy. 'Come back,' you say. I do remember the good times. The feeling of flying high. The feeling of no resistance. I imagine it much like the hawk coasting high in the air, no wind, just the feeling of power, confidence, a pure ancient feeling of being one with the animal you were meant to be. Anorexia is the animal I was meant to be, I know this."

'Then come back.'

"I can feel you, I felt your breath on my neck when I lost weight. That is why you are here, right? That is why we are meeting, why we are close enough to smell each other, close enough to fall into each other, I didn't mean to lose it. You didn't need to come. I planned for you. I knew you would come...all it takes is a few pounds and you are back....hand on my chin, forcing my face to the mirror to inspect, forcing my fingers to keep empty plates...always forcing."

'It feels good, but it feels good, come back.'

"God yes, it does feel good. Already. Just a few glimpses of a smaller body part. Just a few empty plates. It feels good. It feels right. It feels like what I have been running from. Then I wonder why I have been running at all If it feels so good. Why did I run from you? Why did we break up if you are so good and loving and calm and such a perfect lover? Why did I run in the first place."

'You shouldn't have run, come back. I can give you all of those feelings again, you have tasted them, they taste better than food, better than friendship, better than family.'

"Yes they do. These feelings you offer do taste better than food, better than friendship, better than family. At first. At first they do. Like the first hit of crystal meth. You are invincible. Like an ancient power has entered your body and 'you' are the only thing you feel, you only feel yourself, but only the best parts of yourself, shining and amplified so that you fail to see anything other than a glowing perfect being. It's not a conceit that you feel, but it is a fullness of being good, of being human, it is a feeling that you think everyone else already has and that you have been missing....until now. It is a feeling that completes any missing parts of you. A feeling that sustains you, gives you life."

'Yes I am that feeling of life and completeness, come back.'

"I yearn without hesitation to return, and that is why you are always running ahead of me, always knowing where I am. I want those feelings like the hawk wants to soar, it is in my bones, in my brain, in my blood to yearn for you. But I am broken. I am whole millions of years ago, I am broken today."

'I can make you whole if you just return.'

"Yes, you can make me whole today, and for a while. But then I will break again. It will feel so good, for a while, then, it will start cracking, my body will start to crumble and my life will fracture piece by piece. I have been in your arms before, and as it was, I stayed too long, I lingered with you at the cost of my loved ones. I was not meant to be whole today, in this time. Instead, I was meant to feel this ambivalence. I was meant to feel this ambivalence like a wound that is always with me. I realize now that it is ok to feel you. It is ok to touch your fingertips and dip my toe in your water. I am stronger now. I am strong enough to run with you as I run away from you, because I know exactly who you are. I know where you live. I know your tricks and your motives. I was prepared for your return, I was waiting for it. I know how you operate and your favorite words to whisper. And yes, they may lead me to a rendezvous now and again, the kiss of an empty plate, or the stolen glance of a lost pound, but your words and ways will never again entice me back into a relationship. I have loved you more than you'll ever know. I still love you. But, love alone is not enough anymore, because when you love, you kill, and I am finally, finally, alive."

Ugly Sweater Contest

Ugly sweater contests, they happen every year at work. They are a time for our staff to come together and do something fun, laugh at each other, and even bond a little bit. Except for me. I have always hated ugly sweater day, HATED it. Don't get me wrong, I love my job, I love the people I work with. But, I also have an eating disorder, and as such I hate anything that has to do with my body.....and an ugly sweater....well, it would have to go on my body. So, for the last twelve years I have not participated in ugly sweater day. Twelve years have gone by and I have never attempted to join my coworkers in this silly tradition. Why? It's just a sweater after all. One little ugly sweater, for one little day of the year, it can't be that hard can it? Yes, actually, it can. Eating disorders are very peculiar things. They come with strict rules, tight boundaries, and irrational fears. And try as I might each year, my eating disorder would never let me put on an ugly sweater.

You see, I always had to be very careful about what I wore to work each day. It had to fit just right, not too tight, not too loose. I had a very particular set of clothing that my eating disorder would let me wear. These Items were kept just for work and would be picked out the night before, everything would be picked out right down to the socks and underwear. It was also extremely difficult for me to buy a new shirt or pair of pants as then I would have to fight with anorexia over if I could even wear it to work....and usually she won, because she has a couple of rules for my clothing, a couple of very, strict rules.

The first rule is that I must look the thinnest I possibly can at all times. I must only wear certain pants with certain shirts to accentuate my thinness. I have to make sure my thigh gap can be seen between my pants. Nothing, and I mean nothing, can have any bulk to it. Not sweaters, not coats, nothing can have bulk. It all has to lie flat and lean so as to give the illusion of long slender lines. I can't wear baggy shirts, or bulky sweaters, or thick warm socks. My shoes have to be slender, even if they hurt. What is so interesting to me about this rule is that it is in direct opposition to rule number two.

Anorexia's next rule is I can only wear bland colors. This rule is so that I do not draw attention to myself as I am so sickly thin and ugly looking. I can't wear colorful or flashy things. So I wear brown things, with black things, and grey things. The thing that is so odd about this rule is that I absolutely can't draw attention to my body with bright colors or even clothing that might be nice enough for someone to compliment because then they would notice my body. And I feel so much shame about my body, because it is too thin, too sickly, too frail looking. Yet, rule number one demands that I look as thin and sickly as I can. I check myself from every angle to make sure I look as slender as possible. But then rule number two demands that I do not draw attention to my body because at the same time I want it to be seen as thin and sickly, I can't have people noticing I am thin and sickly. This eating disorder shit is fucked up. And it means for the last 12 years I have worn the same things to work. That is, until recovery showed up and my body changed.

Something magical and unexpected happened as I gained weight in recovery. It was actually quite the opposite of what you would expect to happen. I thought (as does everyone with an eating disorder I would assume) that the more weight I gained in recovery the more I would hate my body. I thought for sure it would be unbearable, that I would not be able to see myself in a new larger body, and I would run back to anorexia. Of course, it was hard at first, as I gained anorexia got so loud, she was screaming and yelling at me to stop, to turn around, to run back to her. But then, as I continued to eat through her noise something happened. I stopped caring so much about my body size. I stopped noticing if I had a thigh gap or not. I stopped looking at my body from every angle to find it's thinness. I was able to just be in a body, have a body, fuel a body. As my body grew I needed new clothes and without even realizing what was happening I found myself branching out into some colors and bulky sweaters. I would pick a shirt because I liked the color or look, not for how thin it made my body look. I could wake in the morning and pick clothes that I actually liked and throw them on for work, I was no longer obsessively choosing outfits the night before. I hadn't noticed that all of this snuck up on me....until ugly sweater day.

It was the last week of work before we broke for Christmas and there wasn't a mention yet of the ugly sweater contest. It crossed my mind that due to Covid perhaps we were foregoing the festive day this year....and I actually found myself conflicted about it. On one hand I hated ugly sweater day....let me rephrase that....anorexia hated ugly sweater day. On the other hand, and for some unknown reason, my mother gifted me an ugly sweater just the week before, and it was very, very, ugly. It had puffy black and red sweater arms, glittery puff balls sewn all over, and it stated proudly in gold sequins, "FAB....YULE...OUS." Then on Wednesday an email came out declaring that we should all wear our ugliest sweaters on Friday...there would be no contest...but the consensus was everyone needed some Christmas cheer.

Thank you recovery brain. Thank you therapy. Thank you mom for the sweater. Let me tell you what I was thinking when I read that email. I was not mad, or annoyed, as I usually am when the ugly sweater day notice comes around. Instead, I was looking forward to wearing my new sweater, I was wondering if it was going to be itchy or not, or would I need an undershirt in case I got too hot. I was mentally wandering around my house finding my gingerbread earrings to wear with it. I was thinking about how fun the day would be with my sweater on, instead of just another boring bland brown shirt. I'll also tell you what I wasn't thinking. I wasn't thinking about how bulky it was. I wasn't thinking about what pants I would wear with it so that it would make me leaner. I wasn't worried about wearing color or sequins or weather or not I was noticed. I was definitely not worried about standing out....I mean, I was going to be wearing an ugly sweater after all.

For the past twelve years I thought for sure my clothing choices were because of my personality. I was shy, I didn't want to draw attention to myself, I love the colors brown and black. And you know what, those things are true. I am shy. I don't like attention. I do love brown and black. But I also love my work, I love my peers, I love color, and I love ugly sweaters.

Open Letter To My Dietician

There are so many things I have left to tell you. You see, I was getting better, I was improving, I was eating. I was also seeing you weekly, connecting, listening to your voice of reason, as I hadn't quite found my own yet. Then COVID happened. I retreated into my home and we slowly connected less, until we stopped connecting at all...not because I fell apart, quite the contrary. Instead it was because my retreat seemed to serve my recovery well, I could focus on my eating, on my relationship with myself. It was easier to gain and learn to accept my new body without having to be in the world everyday. You taught me well, and I kept fighting, kept moving, kept growing, and now I have come out the other side with so many moments that I have wanted to share. So many little victories that no one else would understand. So many times have I thought, "wow, I just did that", and then looked around to have no one to share it with. Yes, I have family and they are happy I have come so far in my recovery. Yes, my husband and daughters often see my successes. But, they do not understand like you understood. They do not see what you saw. Often, now, when my voice of reason chimes in to take over from the eating disordered voice, it is your voice that I hear. Your words that you have placed in my brain so that I could use them later to save myself. Thank you for that, and here are some times when I hear your voice or look for you....

I remember the first time I was in your office. I was eating only two foods at the time, bell peppers and spinach. You placed that meal plan pamphlet in front of me, the one with lists of foods under headings such as 'breakfast', 'lunch', or 'snack'. I remember asking if I had to pick one food from each page...already terrified seeing so many fears in front of me....you gently clarified for me that I was to pick multiple exchanges from each heading. I laughed as my eyes focused in on the page to reveal fear food after fear food. I did my best, I ate plates of safe food with minuscule amounts of fear food on top...but slowly the ratio shifted. Today I eat plates upon plates of fear foods. Fear foods with a bit of safe food on top....fear foods with fear foods on the side....fear foods for every meal and snack. And do you know what happened? They stopped being fear foods. They are just foods. There are so many times I look at my plate and feel so proud with my choices...I want to send you pictures and shout out to you, 'look, look, I am doing it, I am doing it', just like a little kid riding a bike for the first time. And you taught me how to ride this bike, you taught me how to eat again, thank you.

Panera opened the other day. You may remember that I used to take mini trips with my daughter a few hours out of town and loved to stop at Panera while there. I could safely fill my belly with carbs at that Panera because I was always prepared to eat due to travel 'restriction' and having it in another town always felt safer than eating carbs in my own town. You loved to tell me that all food is safe food. Food is food, I am allowed. You would tell me all the reasons carbs are good for you, even white carbs, which I truly thought were the enemy. You were right. I am allowed. I am allowed to order all the good stuff. I am allowed to run down to our new Panera with my daughter the day they opened. I am allowed. I ordered breads as bowls, as loaves, as rolls. I ordered sweets as croissants with chocolate, as cookies, and as scones. I picked up my giant bag of carbs with my daughter and when anorexia tried to step in I refused to let her speak. I spoke first. I spoke to my daughter, we spoke about all of the treats and then we sampled them all the way home. We had a bite of this, and a slice of that. We tasted everything. In fact, by the time we got home we were both much too full to have a proper 'snack or meal' out of any of it. I looked at all the breads and treats we spread out on the table. I was full. I was content. I was actually happy. I was not consumed with the carbs in front of me. I could walk away from them, read a book or watch a movie, and actually forget they were there. For the next few days I would walk into the kitchen, and see the Panera slowing shrinking. You told me this would happen, but I didn't believe you. You told me food would lose its power over me, I didn't believe you. Well, I believe you now. You were so right. I can have the bread, I can also walk by the bread. I can forget the bread is there, then be surprised when I see it. But mostly I am surprised that food is now just food. It is no longer taunting me. It is no longer haunting me all day and night. Food is just sitting on the counter these days, and I can eat it if I want, and walk by it if I want. Thank you for this gift. You would be proud.

You used to tell me that everyone that recovers is glad they did, that no one looks back and regrets recovering. I would argue because I could not comprehend that I could be content in a larger body, and we all know it takes a larger body to recover. My body has grown and grown some more, it was painful, it hurt both physically and emotionally. Every few pounds I would panic and want to run back to anorexia, but I put my faith in your experience and knowledge and kept going. I may know anorexia better than you, but you knew recovery better than me. I would come to you with thoughts of, 'how many pounds will come off in the shower if I scrub a layer of skin', or 'I wonder if I can get skinny enough to fit toddler size pant legs.' You never shamed me. You were a safe place to say these thoughts and have them countered, you could be the voice of reason when I couldn't. I have been wanting to tell you that my voice has returned and when it does I think of you. Anorexia still tells me I need to be smaller, but now I can take care of her myself. I remind her that I am a mother, a woman, a wife, and as such I need a larger body. A larger body is not a bad body. I should be larger than my children. I should have curves and fat. My body is more comforting to my family with this extra weight on it. I am content, I am happy. I can run around naked with my husband and feel comfortable in my skin, that is something I thought I would never be able to do, and it is truly a priceless gift of recovery.

I can't begin to tell you all of the times you show up in my life. I think of you when I stand in the kitchen and think 'what do I want to eat', not, 'what can I have'. I think of you whenever I drink liquid calories, smoothies, coffees with real cream, or sweet fruity drinks. I look for you when I fill a plate of food that I never thought I would be able to eat again....and then I eat it without fear or judgment. I think of you when I choose groceries without looking at the labels. I see you when my kids steal food off of my plate because they are not afraid I am going to die without the extra nourishment. Then, I think of all the lies I told you. The lie that I liked americanos better than sweet milky coffees. The lie that mustard on lettuce is a salad, or the lie that I loved roasted veggies without any oils or fats. There were so many lies,

lies to you, lies to myself. You never called me out on all my lies. You just sat with them, gently questioned them with compassion. You taught me how to do the same. You taught me how to show myself compassion, how to question myself when I need to in order to keep moving forward in my recovery, and now I look for you when my voice is using your words.

Now That I Am Size Unknown

Now that I am size unknown I do not feel shame at seeing the number on the scale rise, If I imagine the number rising I fight the shame instead, and it is lessening.

Now that I am size unknown I cry when my pants don't fit, then I buy new pants and wear them out for a nice meal with my husband, we both enjoy a meal better when our pants fit.

Now that I am a size unknown I no longer feel comfort by stroking my bones, instead I feel comfort when I feel my belly and it reminds me that it is safe and normal to eat, real human women have bellies.

Now that I am a size unknown my daughter can tend to her own life instead of worrying for mine.

Now that I am a size unknown my primal fear of bananas has gone.

Now that I am size unknown my body no longer waits for me to sleep so it can rouse me into semi-consciousness, send me to the kitchen, and feed me the calories I refuse during the day.

Now that I am size unknown I can read a book without circling through the same sentence over and over and over.

Now that I am a size unknown my clothes have all types of different numbers on them because I am not a size, I am a body, and bodies fit different numbers. Yes I still mourn the small numbers, but at the same time, the bigger numbers feel like the gift of hard work and peace.

Now that I am a size unknown I don't count calories, Instead I count coffee dates with my daughters or nice meals spent with my husband.

Now that I am size unknown I have space within myself to be there for my children in a way that anorexia never let me.

Now that I am a size unknown I eat cake when I want to, for a while it felt terrifying, now it just feels good.

Now that I am a size unknown I realize I do not want to eat cake all of the time, like I once thought I would, cake does not consume me, food does not consume me, I consume food.

Now that I am a size unknown I miss people looking at my skinny body, but I am also glad no one has to look at my skinny body, it was sick.

Now that I am size unknown I can truly feel the warmth of the sun, instead of the constant shiver of cold.

Now that I am size unknown my children can sleep without fear their mother is dying.

Now that I am a size unknown I miss the good feeling I would get from restricting, but now I feel good when I make my favorite foods and plate them beautifully for myself.

Now that I am size unknown I can try new things, like hot coffee poured over a scoop of vanilla ice cream, or crusty bread dipped in pumpkin vinegar and oil.

Now that I am size unknown I am finally bigger than my children and that feels right.

Now that I am size unknown I can eat food and if it is not perfect I can move on with my day without it tearing me apart inside.

Now that I am a size unknown I can eat. Then I can eat again. Then I can eat again. I can eat. I can eat and it feels wonderful.

Now that I am a size unknown I no longer dream of eating foods and bolt awake worrying that I actually ate them.

Now that I am size unknown I can receive a gift of food and eat some with the gift giver instead of not sharing and throwing it in the garbage. What a gift for the both of us.

Now that I am size unknown I can sit on the couch, in fact, I can sit. I can actually just sit.

Now that I am a size unknown I am sometimes worried about the size of my body, but at the same time I love the size of my body.

Now that I am a size unknown I don't have to look up menus before I go to a restaurant.

Now that I am a size unknown I realize I can eat what I like, I don't have to eat like anyone else, I can just eat like me, and discovering what I like can be challenging but also fun.

Now that I am a size unknown I get scared I will grow bigger and bigger, I might, or I might not, either way I will still be me, me without anorexia.

Now that I am size unknown I have moments where I feel like I have lost my best friend, my safety net, my one thing I was good at, and yes, I may have lost anorexia, but that just means other things can grow, and they are, and they will.

Now that I am a size unknown I can trust my own thoughts, they have come back and are louder than anorexia's.

Now that I am a size unknown I believe all the things my therapist and dietitian told me when I thought they were lying.

Now that I am a size unknown I am strong, I am happy, I am content.

Now that I am a size unknown I will not die of anorexia.

Printed in Great Britain
by Amazon